PROVERBS:
Principles of Wisdom

PROVERBS:
Principles of Wisdom

by
Bob Yandian

HARRISON HOUSE
Tulsa, Oklahoma

Unless otherwise indicated,
all Scripture quotations are taken from
the *King James Version* of the Bible.

Cover photograph by Saul Shuster

4th Printing
Over 25,000 in Print

PROVERBS: Principles of Wisdom
ISBN O-89274-386-7
Copyright © 1985 by Bob Yandian
P. O. Box 35842
Tulsa, Oklahoma 74153

Published by Harrison House, Inc.
P. O. Box 35035
Tulsa, Oklahoma 74153

Printed in the United States of America.

Table of Contents

Foreword

Many Christians today are full of the "in Him" truths. They are quick to acknowledge and confess all that they are—and what all they know!—now that they belong to Christ. They give the appearance of being filled to overflowing with knowledge about righteousness, healing, salvation and Christian authority. To listen to them talk, you would think they were virtual repositories of spiritual truth. Yet for all their supposed spiritual knowledge, many of these same people seem to be totally foolish and unlearned when it comes to the natural, everyday things of life. And as James would say, "My brethren, these things ought not so to be" (James 3:10).

As Christians, we live in two worlds: natural and supernatural. Even with all our great spiritual knowledge, we still have to live out our daily lives on this earth. We still have to make a living, for example. The "righteousness of God" still has to sweep the floor, carry out the garbage and change the oil in the car. The "joint-heir with Christ" still has to fix meals and mow the yard. All these marvelous prosperity and protection truths we are learning about today are a reality. But as true as they are, we still need to have wisdom in the natural, everyday things of life.

That's where the book of Proverbs, the subject of this study, comes in. It is a prime reference source for wisdom in the practical, "nitty-gritty" details of daily existence. Its primary human author is Solomon, the greatest man of wisdom recorded in the Word of God, apart from Jesus Christ Himself. That's why a study of his writings is so well worth our time and attention.

In our study of Proverbs we will be considering different topics in it, rather than making a verse-by-verse analysis of it. Since there are 31 chapters in the book of Proverbs, I would suggest that you start reading one chapter each day beginning on the first day of the month. That way, you will basically cover the whole book once each month. Reading Proverbs regularly will build into your life the wisdom of God. Just think of the result of reading it through twelve times in the span of one year! If you will take the time to plant into your mind the wisdom of God, you will reap a harvest of blessings. When you face difficult situations, the Holy Spirit will bring to your remembrance some verse that will enable you to deal wisely in all the affairs of life.

Whence Cometh Wisdom?—

"But where shall wisdom be found? and where is the place of understanding?

"Man knoweth not the price thereof; neither is it found in the land of the living.

"The depth saith, It is not in me: and the sea saith, It is not with me.

"It cannot be gotten for gold, neither shall silver be weighed for the price thereof.

"It cannot be valued with the gold of Ophir, with the precious onyx, or the sapphire.

"The gold and the crystal cannot equal it: and the exchange of it shall not be for jewels of fine gold.

"No mention shall be made of coral, or of pearls: for the price of wisdom is above rubies.

"The topaz of Ethiopia shall not equal it, neither shall it be valued with pure gold.

"Whence then cometh wisdom? and where is the place of understanding?

"Seeing it is hid from the eyes of all living, and kept close from the fowls of the air.

"Destruction and death say, We have heard the fame thereof with our ears.

"God understandeth the way thereof, and he knoweth the place thereof.

"For he looketh to the ends of the earth, and seeth under the whole heaven;

"To make the weight for the winds; and he weigheth the waters by measure.

"When he made a decree for the rain, and a way for the lightning of the thunder:

"Then did he see it, and declare it; he prepared it, yea, and searched it out.

"And unto man he said, Behold, the fear of the Lord, that is wisdom; and to depart from evil is understanding" (Job 28:12-28).

As an introduction to our study, let's consider what Job had to say about this vital and timely subject of wisdom.

"Man knoweth not the price thereof; neither is it found in the land of the living" (v. 13.) In this verse Job points out man's inability to find wisdom on his own. We must quit looking to man for wisdom because man looks to nature for his wisdom.

"The depth saith, It is not in me: and the sea saith, It is not with me" (v. 14). But Job tells us that wisdom is not to be found in nature. Nor can it be purchased. (v. 15.)

"God understandeth the way thereof, and he knoweth the place thereof" (v. 23). Notice that GOD is the one who knows all about wisdom.

"And unto man he said, Behold, the fear of the Lord, that is wisdom; and to depart from evil is understanding" (v. 28). Job points out that wisdom is actually the fear or reverence of the Lord.

The first thing we must do to have wisdom is to recognize that all wisdom comes from God. We cannot see God with our physical eye, but the Bible says that God became flesh; Jesus was the Word made flesh. (John 1:14.) So if we want to know where wisdom is to be found, it is in God's Word. If we want to become wise, we must reverence God's Word. Because the Word of God IS God.

Knowledge and Wisdom—

PROVERBS 1:1-7
The proverbs of Solomon the son of David, king of Israel;

To know wisdom and instruction; to perceive the words of understanding;

To receive the instruction of wisdom, justice, and judgment, and equity;

To give subtilty to the simple, to the young man knowledge and discretion.

A wise man will hear, and will increase learning; and a man of understanding shall attain unto wise counsels:

To understand a proverb, and the interpretation; the words of the wise, and their dark sayings.

The fear of the Lord is the beginning of knowledge: but fools despise wisdom and instruction.

Knowledge and wisdom are two different things: Knowledge is *taking in* the Word of God; wisdom is *putting out* the Word of God. Knowledge is the *accumulation* of facts; wisdom is the correct *application* of those facts. But notice in verse seven that Solomon says that knowledge comes from the reverence of the Lord. Knowledge and wisdom both begin by reverencing the Word of God. If you want to be knowledgeable, *study* God's Word. If you want to be wise, *apply* God's Word. If you will do both of these two things, you will be successful in all areas of your life.

"The proverbs of Solomon the son of David, king of Israel" (v. 1) These proverbs were written down as Solomon's remembrance of what his father David had taught him. Now David began to teach Solomon after the death of his son Absalom. David failed with his first two sons, Adonijah and Absalom. He did not teach them the things that had made him a success.

Only after failing with his first two children did David learn to pass on his knowledge and wisdom to Solomon. But Solomon did not follow suit. That's the sad part: David shared his knowledge and wisdom with Solomon, but Solomon failed to pass it on. Solomon had a son named Rehoboam who ended up destroying the kingdom he had inherited from his father. Solomon had great knowledge and wisdom, but he neglected to instruct his house in the ways of the Lord. As a result of his negligence, not only his family but an entire kingdom was lost. That's why it is so important for us today to find wisdom, and to pass it on to future generations.

So often when we become successful in the Word of God, we become just a bit too proud to share the secret of that success with others. After all, we did it by ourselves; let them do the same! That is not right. We should be open to share with others those promises from the Word that made us a success; we need to teach our brothers and sisters how they can obtain the same results we did. Especially should we be open to share with our own children. We should pass on from generation to generation what the Word of God has done for us.

Wisdom is built upon wisdom. If we will be diligent to carefully instruct our children in the knowledge and wisdom which was passed down to us from our fathers, God can take that foundation and build upon it. Our offspring can become even wiser than we are. And their children will be wiser than they.

Wisdom is as infinite as God Himself. As we increase in it, it increases in us. It can be passed on from age to age, growing and expanding with each succeeding generation.

The word "proverb" actually refers to a rule or a standard. In Hebrew it means "to be like." So who is it we are to be like? God. These are the proverbs (rules, standards) of God Himself, passed down to us through Solomon. If we want to be like God, the best way to do that is through study and application of His Word. That's what it's given to us for!

When a gardener wants a tender young tomato plant to grow up strong and straight, he doesn't say to it, "Now plant, I want you to grow up straight. But I'm leaving that up to you. You just grow up any way you feel is right for you." If he is foolish enough to do that, most likely he will not harvest many good tomatoes. Left on its own, that plant will grow in whatever direction offers the least resistance. It will fall down and spread out in all directions. Any good vegetable gardener will tell you that young tomato plants have to have a firm support as they grow and develop. That's why a strong stake is driven into the ground next to each plant and attached to it, to serve as a guide and support for its growth.

So it is with our children. If we want them to grow up tall and straight morally and spiritually, we must provide them some standard that does not change. We dare not leave them to choose their own standard, or allow them to live their lives without one. Many voices in our society today would have us turn our children totally loose to choose and set their own standards. That is not only foolish, it is in direct opposition to the Word of God. In Proverbs 22:15, wise Solomon tells us: "Foolishness is bound in the heart of a child; but the rod of correction shall drive it far from him."

The Word of God and discipline will keep our children from foolishness. So, what are we to do with "these kids today"? How do we insure that all these flexible, pliant young "plants" grow up tall and straight in the Lord? We put down our stake. We bind those youngsters to a rule or standard that will not change.

The Word of God is eternal. Like God Himself, His Word remains forever the same. (Heb. 13:8.) If we will take the time and effort to bind our children to the Word of God, if we will train them up in the way they should go, then when they are old, they will not depart from it. That is a promise from God! (Prov. 22:6.)

The Wisdom of Solomon—

"And God gave Solomon wisdom and understanding exceeding much, and largeness of heart, even as the sand that is on the sea shore.

"And Solomon's wisdom excelled the wisdom of all the children of the east country, and all the wisdom of Egypt.

"For he was wiser than all men; than Ethan the Ezrahite, and Heman, and Chalcol, and Darda, the sons of Mahol: and his fame was in all nations round about.

"And he spake three thousand proverbs: and his songs were a thousand and five.

"And he spake of trees, from the cedar tree that is in Lebanon even unto the hyssop that springeth out of the wall: he spake also of beasts, and of fowl, and of creeping things, and of fishes.

"And there came of all people to hear the wisdom of Solomon, from all kings of the earth, which had heard of his wisdom" (1 Kings 4:29-34).

"And he spake three thousand proverbs: and his songs were a thousand and five" (v. 32). Solomon was a tremendously

gifted and talented man. There seems to have been almost no limit to his creative ability. If he wrote three thousand proverbs, that means that we only have a portion of them recorded in the 31 chapters of the book of Proverbs. Obviously the Lord chose out only the best for our benefit. But these are more than sufficient for the development of wisdom. As you and I fill our minds and hearts with them, there is no telling what will come forth from our mouths!

In Ephesians 5:18,19 the Apostle Paul exhorted us: "And be not drunk with wine, wherein is excess; but be filled with the Spirit; speaking to yourselves in psalms and hymns and spiritual songs, singing and making melody in your heart to the Lord." Can you imagine a thousand and five new songs? In Colossians 3:16 Paul wrote: "Let the word of Christ dwell in you richly in all *wisdom*; teaching and admonishing one another in psalms and hymns and spiritual songs, singing with grace in your hearts to the Lord." Solomon was a living fulfillment of this scripture; it seems clear that he had become so full of the Word of God that every time he opened his mouth, out came songs and words of wisdom! And so it will be with US too, if we will fill our heart and mind with God's Holy Word.

"And he spake of trees, from the cedar tree that is in Lebanon even unto the hyssop that springeth out of the wall: he spake also of beasts, and of fowl, and of creeping things, and of fishes" (v. 33). This verse is a capsule outline of the book of Proverbs. Cedar trees are great things, hyssop is very small. They represent the two extremes of the full spectrum of Solomon's wide field of knowledge and wisdom. As we read and learn his words, we too will become wise in things both great and small.

"And there came of all people to hear the wisdom of Solomon, from all kings of the earth, which had heard of his wisdom" (v. 34). Don't you think it is a wise idea for us to study Proverbs if the kings of his day journeyed from the four corners of the earth to hear Solomon's wisdom? Do you not feel that

he qualifies as a teacher worth heeding? It would have been nice to have been able to personally sit at the feet of Solomon as he composed and quoted his songs and words of wisdom. Yet we have been given an even greater Teacher: "The queen of the south shall rise up in judgment with this generation, and shall condemn it: for she came from the uttermost parts of the earth to hear the wisdom of Solomon; and behold, a greater than Solomon is here" (Matt. 12:42). And, according to 1 Corinthians 1:30, this same JESUS who spoke these words concerning Himself was MADE UNTO US wisdom.

The Source of Solomon's Wisdom—

"And Solomon went up thither to the brasen altar before the Lord, which was at the tabernacle of the congregation, and offered a thousand burnt offerings upon it.

"In that night did God appear unto Solomon, and said unto him, Ask what I shall give thee.

"And Solomon said unto God, Thou hast shewed great mercy unto David my father, and hast made me king over a people like the dust of the earth in multitude.

"Give me now wisdom and knowledge, that I may go out and come in before this people: for who can judge this thy people, that is so great?

"And God said to Solomon, Because this was in thine heart, and thou hast not asked riches, wealth, or honour, nor the life of thine enemies, neither yet hast asked long life; but hast asked wisdom and knowledge for thyself, that thou mayest judge my people, over whom I have made thee king:

"Wisdom and knowledge is granted unto thee; and I will give thee riches, and wealth, and honour, such as none of the kings have had that have been before thee, neither shall there any after thee have the like" (2 Chron. 1:6-12).

"*And Solomon went up...before the Lord...and offered a thousand burnt offerings...*" (v. 6). Many people ask me why

God has never appeared to them. I usually answer that question with a question: "When was the last time you offered up sacrifices to Him?" Notice that God appeared to Solomon AFTER he had offered up to Him a thousand burnt offerings. Solomon didn't do this to cause God to shew Himself; he did it simply because he loved the Lord. He was so grateful for all that God had done for him that he just wanted to praise and honor Him for who He is. Sacrifice appeals to God; it tugs on His heart strings. But under the New Covenant we no longer offer up burnt sacrifices; instead, we are told by the Apostle Paul what our "reasonable service" is—to offer our own bodies as "a living sacrifice, holy, acceptable unto God" (Rom. 12:1). In John 14:21 the Lord Jesus told us: "He that hath my commandments, and keepeth them, he it is that loveth me: and he that loveth me shall be loved of my Father, and I will love him, and will manifest myself to him." To those who truly love the Lord and keep His commandments, He appears all the time; they just don't always recognize Him.

"Give me now wisdom and knowledge..." (v. 10). Notice that the way Solomon got wisdom was by ASKING for it. James tells us: "If any of you lack wisdom, let him *ask* of God, that giveth to all men liberally, and upbraideth not and it shall be given him" (James 1:5). If we need wisdom for our everyday lives, we should begin by doing just what Solomon did—*ask God for it*. That's where wisdom comes from. Notice that Solomon didn't ask men for it. Job has already told us that wisdom doesn't come from men. It has been hidden from them. True wisdom comes from God.

"...Because this was in thine heart...., I will give thee riches, and wealth, and honour..." (vv. 11,12). The final point from this passage is God's graciousness. When Solomon asked for wisdom and knowledge, he also received riches, wealth, honor and long life. He had sought for a higher thing from God, but received these blessings as well. That should remind us of another promise from the Lord: "But seek ye

first the kingdom of God, and his righteousness; and all these things shall be added unto you" (Matt. 6:33). The same promise is given to us today as was given to Solomon in ancient Israel. Shouldn't we believe it and act on it as he did?

Two Kinds of Wisdom—

PROVERBS 3:13-17

Happy is the man that findeth wisdom, and the man that getteth understanding.

For the merchandise of it is better than the merchandise of silver, and the gain thereof than fine gold.

She is more precious than rubies: and all the things thou canst desire are not to be compared unto her.

Length of days is in her right hand; and in her left hand riches and honour.

Her ways are ways of pleasantness, and all her paths are peace.

"Happy is the man that findeth wisdom..." (v. 13). Notice that although wisdom comes from God, the man who gets wisdom has to search for it. It doesn't just fall on him.

"She is more precious than rubies..." (v. 15). Notice also that wisdom is referred to as "she." This theme will be carried on throughout the book of Proverbs. Wisdom is continually referred to as a beautiful and virtuous woman. We will also see that, by way of contrast, man's wisdom is always presented as a harlot.

"Length of days is in her right hand; and in her left hand riches and honour" (v. 16). Again in this passage, as in 2 Chronicles, we see that riches, honor and long life accompany the wisdom of God. But yet we are told not to seek after riches and health and long life for their own sake, but rather to seek after wisdom, then all these other things will be added to us.

"Length of days is in her right hand; and in her left riches and honour" (v. 17). Notice that wisdom comes equipped with two hands: one holds riches and honor and the other length of days. Notice too that the riches and honor are in her LEFT hand while length of days is in her RIGHT hand.

Usually we think of the right hand as the predominant hand, the hand of honor. For example, Jesus is seated at the right hand of God. (Col. 3:1.) In Matthew 25:33 Jesus speaks of setting the sheep (the righteous) on His right hand, but the goats (the unrighteous) on His left hand. Now there is nothing inherently wrong with the left hand. But it is true that one hand is used more often and with greater dexterity than the other. For most people, that is the right hand, the more honored hand. Remember in Matthew 5:29 where Jesus counseled His disciples, "If thy right eye offend thee...; if thy right hand offend thee..."? So the right hand is the predominant one.

Notice that in the predominant hand is length of days, while riches and honor are in the left. We should get our priorities straight: health and long life are really greater than all the wealth and fame of this world. How many people today would give all their earthly treasure and notoriety for good health or for just one more year of life?

The Source of Wisdom—

"Only be thou strong and very courageous, that thou mayest observe to do according to all the law, which Moses my servant commanded thee: turn not from it to the right hand or to the left, that thou mayest prosper whithersoever thou goest" (Josh. 1:7).

"...turn not from it to the right hand or to the left...." Notice that Joshua is instructed not to turn to the right *hand* nor to the left. Wisdom does come equipped with two hands, but we are not to turn either to one of those hands or to the other in pursuit of what they hold. Many people start

out seeking wisdom and end up pursuing what she holds. Just as many other people start out seeking after the Word of God and end up seeking prosperity, or physical healing, or success, or some other tangible benefit of the Word. Don't do that! Seek first the kingdom of God and His righteousness (that which is intangible and invisible) and then all these tangible and visible things—the left and right hand—will be added to you, just as God has promised in His Word!

In 3 John 2 we read these words: "Beloved, I wish above all things that thou mayest prosper and be in health, even as thy soul prospereth." Notice the contents of the right and left hands again. If you seek after wisdom with all your heart, the contents of these two hands come free of charge. Therefore, seek after wisdom. Pursue it. Read, study, meditate in the Word of God, the source of God's wisdom. Is there any limit to the prosperity of the soul? Then there is no limit to how much God will prosper you in this life.

"...that thou mayest prosper whithersoever thou goest." If you will seek after wisdom for her own sake, God has promised to prosper you no matter what direction your search may take you. Never be afraid of following the ways of the Lord, for His paths "are peace" (Prov. 3:17). The Psalmist says that God's paths "drop fatness" (Ps. 65:11).

There are five different Hebrew words for wisdom. Let's look at the one that is used most frequently. It is the one which appears in Proverbs 1:2: "To know *wisdom* and instruction; to perceive the words of understanding." The Hebrew word translated "wisdom" in this verse is *chokmah*, the root meaning of which has to do with pounding something in. In order to have the wisdom of God, it is necessary to "pound in" knowledge into your head and heart. You have to read, study and (especially) meditate in the Word of God. Day and night. Night and day. The more you meditate, the more you pound in.

That's why it is so important to read the Word of God daily. Once you have read a chapter, you should ask the

Spirit of the Lord to call up to your mind certain scriptures from that chapter so you can meditate upon them again and again. That way the scriptures become yours—God's message to you individually and personally.

Studying the Word is like learning the multiplication tables. You didn't learn that seven times eight equals fifty-six by simply hearing or reading that fact one time; you memorized it. You went over and over those tables, time after time, pounding them into your mind and spirit. So it is with the Word of God. Just reading it once is not enough. You need to dwell on it, meditate on it, memorize it, digest it, pound it in—until it becomes a part of you. Until you not only remember it—you can't forget it!

When that happens, you will never forget that in wisdom's left hand are riches and honor, and in her right hand is length of days. More than that, you will begin to find what you set out to seek—the wisdom of God!

Introduction:
Types of Proverbs

Many of the proverbs of Solomon make sense naturally; it's not difficult to understand them. We grasp their meaning right away and our own experience tells us that they are true. Others will be more difficult to understand and to relate to our modern-day lifestyle. Not only because of the difference in our modern culture from that of ancient Israel, but also because of the "language barrier" of the *King James* Bible.

Proverbs are more than just simple sayings. They are the very wisdom of God expressed in the everyday language of man. To understand the words then is not enough; as with all scripture, we must get past the words of men into the mind of God.

Therefore, in order to truly appreciate and benefit from the truths expressed in these proverbs, we will need the presence of God's own Holy Spirit to reveal to us the *wisdom* contained (and often hidden) in these "wise sayings."

There are six basic types of proverbs that we will be studying in this chapter as part of the groundwork we must lay before actually getting into the themes presented in this book.

Type 1—

The first type of proverb is called *synonymous*. We know the word synonym which refers to two words which have basically the same meaning. A synonymous proverb then is one in which both lines say essentially the same thing but expressed in a slightly different way. An example is Proverbs 11:15: "The liberal soul shall be made fat: and he that watereth shall be watered also himself."

This is a verse on prosperity. It is saying that those who truly become prosperous are givers, because generosity is an attitude of the heart, an attitude which results in blessing.

Another example is Proverbs 11:29: "He that troubleth his own house shall inherit the wind: and the fool shall be servant to the wise of heart." Anyone who doesn't know how to manage his own household will eventually lose everything he has. He will end up inheriting the wind, which is nothing but vanity and vexation of spirit. Who will then "inherit" his goods, the possession of the fool? The wise, of course.

It has been claimed that Communism is not so bad because its primary purpose is simply to insure that all the wealth of this world is equally divided among all the inhabitants of the earth so that all possess the same amount of good things. That does sound good. In theory. But in practice, it just won't work. Even if it were possible to take all the material wealth of this earth, divide it up and distribute it evenly among all the people around the globe, it still wouldn't work. Because it wouldn't stay evenly distributed. Within a few years the smart ones would have it all back again. Some people are just fools when it comes to money. Some shrewd operator would soon dupe them into turning over to him everything they own.

This proverb then warns against being foolish in managing our household affairs. Otherwise we will end up as a servant to the wise in heart.

In each of these proverbs, the same basic idea is expressed in both parts of the verse. These are synonymous proverbs.

Type 2—

The second type of proverb is called *antithetical*. This simply means that a thought is presented in the first line, with the negative of that thought expressed in the second line. Many times the theme of an antithetical proverb is basically this: "If you do such and such, you will be blessed; but if you don't, this is what will happen." So the negative line really accentuates the positive one.

Let's look at Proverbs 14:30 for example: "A sound heart is the life of the flesh: but envy the rottenness of the bones." (You'll always find a "but" somewhere in an antithetical proverb—usually between the first and second lines— because two things are being contrasted.) We believers ought to have the healthiest flesh of anyone on this earth, because our heart is full of the joy of the Lord. And a sound heart is the life of the flesh. But the opposite of that is also true. Envy is the rottenness of the bones. When we get off into strife and discord, we open the door for Satan to come in and put sickness and disease on us.

Consider Proverbs 17:22: "A merry heart doeth good like a medicine: but a broken spirit drieth the bones." This proverb says essentially the same thing as the one above. Why do you think Solomon mentioned this thought twice within three chapters? Did he perhaps forget that he had already made this statement? Or was it because he knew that wisdom had to be *pounded in*? Repetition is the key to learning.

The Apostle Peter obviously knew this principle because in 2 Peter 1:12 he wrote: "Wherefore I will not be negligent to put you always in remembrance of these things, though ye know them, and be established in the present truth." In other words, he was saying, "I know you've probably heard all this fifty times or more, but here it is again. It doesn't bother me to remind you of what you already know and are established in." Which evokes the words of Paul in his letter to the believers in Philippi: "Finally, my brethren, rejoice in the Lord. To write the same things to you, to me indeed is not grievous, but for you it is safe" (Phil. 3:1). Paul didn't mind repeating himself because he knew it was necessary for people to hear the truth repeatedly.

So in this study we will be mentioning many things over and over again, reiterating, repeating, reviewing, so that the truth will be driven deep into our mind and heart.

Type 3—

Let's look at the third type of proverb. This is probably the rarest of all types in the book of Proverbs. It's called a *synthetic* proverb. The name is derived from the word "synthesis" which Webster defines as a "composition or combination of parts, elements, etc., so as to form a whole" (*Webster's New Collegiate Dictionary*). This term is used to identify a proverb in which both lines seem to express a totally different thought (even sometimes direct opposites), yet which have one common theme.

An example is Proverbs 10:18: "He that hideth hatred with lying lips, and he that uttereth a slander, is a fool." In this scripture, the first line deals with lying or falsehood, while the second line concerns slander or malicious talk. One speaker hides his true feelings; the other speaker makes no attempt to conceal his. Although the actions are direct opposites, both are condemned because the intent and results are the same—harm and injury. The common theme is, of course, wrong use of the tongue.

This is a theme which cannot be overly emphasized. Someone has said that the best way to avoid "losing face" is to keep the lower half of it shut! That is basically true. We seldom regret having said too little. But how often have we "kicked ourselves" for "opening our big fat mouth"!

For example, if we dislike someone, if we disagree violently with him, that is a good time to keep our mouth securely fastened! We should hold our peace and deal with our emotions on the inside. If we find ourselves about to slander someone, the wise thing to do is to keep our tongue in check.

Yet there are times when we should speak. The wisdom here is knowing when to open our mouth and when to keep it closed. A fool has no such discretion. He speaks up loud and clear when he should be silent; and he "clams up" just when he should use his mouth for a positive witness and blessing.

Type 4—

The fourth type of proverb is called an *integral* proverb. In this type, the second line completes the thought of the first line. Because the thought flows so well, the effect produced is almost that of one continuous line with no interruption. There are many of this type in the book of Proverbs. For example, Proverbs 13:14: "The law of the wise is a fountain of life, to depart from the snares of death." Here the second line completes or complements the thought of the first.

Consider also Proverbs 19:20: "Hear counsel, and receive instruction, that thou mayest be wise in thy latter end." The second line emphasizes the results obtained by applying the first.

Oh, that children would learn this verse! Not just memorize it, but learn to put it into practice. If they don't listen now while they are young, there will come a day when they will wish they had listened. Yet they don't seem to realize that fact. And it's so hard for parents to communicate that truth to them. It's amazing how stupid and ignorant parents sometimes become when their children get to be teenagers! Mark Twain is reported to have noted, "When I was 17 I thought my father was the most ignorant man I had ever known; but then when I got to be 21, I was amazed at how much the old fellow had learned in only four short years!"

Proverbs says that it is important to hear counsel and receive instruction. Because that is the best way to insure success in the future. If that is true for adults, how much more does it apply to youth. If you are a young person still at home, learn from the Word of God. Listen to the instructions of your parents. "Be not wise in your own conceits" (Rom. 12:16.)

Proverbs 22:6 counsels parents: "Train up a child in the way he should go: and when he is old, he will not depart from it." This is another example of an integral proverb. Notice the word "the." The world would say that there are *many* ways to train up a child, but wise Solomon declares that there is only *one* way: God's way. And God's way of training up a child is by His Word.

Proverbs 22:10 tells us: "Cast out the scorner, and contention shall go out; yea, strife and reproach shall cease." Are you faced with strife and reproach? It is probably because you are being scorned by someone. If you will get rid of the scorner, then that contention, strife and reproach will go out with him.

Type 5—

The fifth kind of proverb is called *parabolic*. In a parabolic proverb the first line illustrates the second. The second line is the teaching, the first is an analogy. Many of these parables do not seem to make sense to the modern mind. Look at Proverbs 11:22 for instance: "As a jewel of gold in a swine's snout, so is a fair woman which is without discretion." We might ask, "What does a piece of gold in a pig's nose have to do with a woman without discretion?"

To the ancient Hebrew, steeped for generations in the law of Moses, nothing was more degraded or contemptible than a hog. Besides being ugly and smelly, to the Jew it was actually profane. Not only were the Hebrews forbidden to eat pork, they would not even touch a swine. Therefore Solomon chose this image of a pig with a gold ring in its snout to symbolize what was to him at the same time the most useless and most repugnant thing imaginable—a beautiful woman with no sense!

Young people would do well to pay attention to what Solomon is saying here. Did you know that if you date someone simply because they are attractive, you are more interested in *you* than you are in *them*? All you're really wanting is something good looking to hang on your arm, just as you would hang an expensive chain around your neck or gold earrings from your ears. That person is nothing more to you than an ornament to enhance your esteem in your own eyes and the eyes of others.

Another parabolic proverb is Proverbs 25:25: "As cold waters to a thirsty soul, so is good news from a far country." Whenever you are far away for any length of time, the best thing you can get is a call from home. It's like a good drink of water to a thirsty soul.

Look at Proverbs 26:9: "As a thorn goeth up into the hand of a drunkard, so is a parable in the mouth of fools." Have you ever seen a drunk hurt himself? Somehow they never seem to feel the pain. They may be involved in a terrible collision that totally demolishes their car and the other driver's, yet somehow they always seem to escape with only minor injuries. And even when they are hurt, their senses are so deadened by alcohol they don't feel the pain. Until they sober up. Then they hurt! It is terrible to see drunkards harm themselves; they don't feel anything, but everyone around them hurts for them.

This proverb is saying, "Just as the senses of a drunkard are too dull to register pain, so are the senses of a fool too dull to register shame. Neither realizes his sad situation and desperate need. And neither understands that he is the cause of his own sorry state."

Proverbs 20:26 states: "Where no wood is, there the fire goeth out: so where there is no talebearer, the strife ceaseth." Does that prick your conscience a bit? If so, you're beginning to get wise.

Type 6—

The final type of proverb is the *comparative* proverb. As its title suggests, a comparative proverb is one which compares one thing with another to illustrate a common trait or theme. For example, Proverbs 27:15: "A continual dropping in a very rainy day and a contentious woman are alike." Have you ever been in a house with a leaky roof during a rainstorm? The steady dripping gets on your nerves, doesn't it? So does the continual nagging of a shrewish wife. What Solomon was saying here is that nagging is not the way to change a person. If you want to change someone, don't nag them to death—love them to life!

In some comparative proverbs the first line expresses something which is superior to or more desirable than the second. The key word in this type of proverb is the word "better." For instance, Proverbs 15:16: "Better is a little with the fear of the Lord than great treasure and trouble therewith." My friend, the prosperity message is great, but if you lose your peace and happiness in the pursuit of wealth, what have you really gained? It's better to possess fewer of this world's goods and a healthy reverence and fear of the Lord than it is to have great earthly treasure and trouble.

Proverbs 10:22 repeats this thought: "The blessing of the Lord, it maketh rich, and he addeth no sorrow with it." When God gives blessings and riches, they do not bring sorrow as they so often do when amassed by worldly means.

Another comparative proverb is Proverbs 15:17: "Better is a dinner of herbs where love is, than a stalled ox and hatred therewith." In other words, it is better to come home from work to a dinner of vegetables and a loving wife, than it is to come home to a filet mignon and a house full of hatred and animosity.

This same idea is repeated in Proverbs 17:1: "Better is a dry morsel, and quietness therewith, than an house full of sacrifices with strife." Wife, when you first married your husband, it's likely you devoted a lot of thought and effort to pleasing your new mate. You probably wanted to be sure to learn to make biscuits like those his mother made for him, or fry chicken just the way he liked it, or whip up his favorite dessert for him. All that is well and good. You should still want to please your husband that way. But none of those things will necessarily make him appreciate you any more, nor will they keep him faithful to you. Despite what you may have heard, the way to a man's heart is not through his stomach; there is another route that is much more direct—and much more effective!

Just remember: Your husband didn't marry you for your cooking! He wasn't looking for a cook; he was looking for a *lover*! You just be the best lover in the world and the cooking will take care of itself. Have you ever heard anyone say, "I'm divorcing my wife because of her apple pie"? I seriously doubt it. It's not food that breaks up homes, it's strife. And the cure for strife is love.

Proverbs 21:9: "It is better to dwell in a corner of the house top, than with a brawling woman in a wide house." With all this teaching on prosperity these days, we are always seeking for bigger houses. We all want one with a *three*-car garage this time. We should have the good sense to quit working on the house, and start building the home. No matter how grand or expensive it may be, no house is worth having if it is devoid of love. Love transforms a cottage into a castle.

Proverbs as Poetry—

So these are the different types of Proverbs. As you read through a chapter of the book each day, try to distinguish the different kinds you are reading. These verses were not just thrown together. There is an order to them, a reason for their placement. They were chosen and arranged to create a flow, like poetry. In fact, that's what a proverb really is:

a two-line poem. In the original Hebrew, the book of Proverbs was a book of poetry as well as a book of wisdom.

As we read through this book, we will see many types of analogies. It's good to keep these scriptures straight and to realize that there is a rhyme and reason to them. Some of them are quite serious; others are delightfully hilarious in their original version. Translated into English, many times they seem to lose much of their humor so only the solemnity is left. That's why we will attempt to highlight the meaning of the original Hebrew as we go along.

1

God's Wisdom Vs. Man's Wisdom
Proverbs 1:1-7; 9:7-9

From this time on we will begin to study certain themes in the book of Proverbs. We will be comparing wisdom with foolishness, and the wisdom of God with the wisdom of the world.

In our study three words will be used quite often. These three words are: knowledge, understanding, and wisdom. We need to distinguish between each of these three terms. Two of these we have already defined. We said that knowledge is the accumulation of facts, and wisdom is the application of those facts. Understanding refers to the ability to arrange facts.

We also noted that the Hebrew word *chokmah*, which is translated "wisdom," actually has to do with "pounding in." This type of wisdom is the kind which comes from applying the Word of God to the experiences of life.

You see, we have two teachers. One teacher is the Word of God and the other teacher is experience. We have always heard that experience is the best teacher. That is not totally true. We can and do learn from our experiences, of course, but experience is not necessarily the BEST way to learn. There is another school besides the "School of Hard Knocks." It is the School of the Holy Spirit. And the primary textbook of this school is the Word of God.

Experience alone is not enough to teach us wisdom. Everyone has experiences, but not everyone profits from them. It is the Word of God which we use IN the experiences of life which actually teaches us wisdom. The Word is like a nail, and experience is like a hammer, driving that nail home. The harder the experience, the more we should lean on the Word and the more wisdom is driven down into our hearts. One day it becomes an inseparable part of us.

Wisdom and Instruction—

PROVERBS 1:1-7

The proverbs of Solomon the son of David, king of Israel;

To know wisdom and instruction; to perceive the words of understanding;

To receive the instruction of wisdom, justice, and judgment, and equity;

To give subtility to the simple, to the young man knowledge and discretion.

A wise man will hear, and will increase learning; and a man of understanding shall attain unto wise counsels:

To understand a proverb, and the interpretation; the words of the wise, and their dark sayings.

The fear of the Lord is the beginning of knowledge: but fools despise wisdom and instruction.

"To know wisdom and instruction..." (v. 2a). This word translated "instruction" is actually the Hebrew word for discipline. Did you know there is a discipline that accompanies learning? It's a discipline to turn off the TV and open up the Bible. It's a discipline to lay down the magazine and turn on the tape player and listen to the Word. The discipline to roll out of bed an hour early in order to devote time to prayer and meditation. The discipline to read and study the Word of God when there are a hundred other things you had rather do. And the devil will always see to it that there is something else to do. Either something more appealing

or else something you feel really needs to be taken care of right away. Usually these things are not tremendously great or important, just the million and one details of everyday life. If you allow him the opportunity, Satan will "nickel and dime" you right into the ground. So take time for the Word of God. MAKE time, if you have to. Wisdom IS a discipline.

"...to *perceive* the words of understanding" (v. 2b). This immediately shows us something. The wisdom of God does not come through natural intellect. Which part of your being do you perceive with? Your spirit. Paul tells us, "But the natural man receiveth not the things of the Spirit of God: for they are foolishness unto him: neither can he know them, because they are spiritually discerned" (1 Cor. 2:14). The things of God are not conceived intellectually, they are perceived spiritually.

Wouldn't it be nice to know that you could walk into any situation in life and be able to perceive the right and wrong of it? With the wisdom of God that is possible. Have you ever found yourself in some situation, perhaps in the company of a friend, and somehow you could sense right off that something was amiss? Perhaps your friend felt nothing at all, but you *knew* that things were just not what they seemed, that something was wrong. That is the kind of spiritual sensitivity all of us should exhibit in the situations of our lives.

The discipline of putting the Word of God into your heart causes you to become so sensitive you can be around people and sense "what manner of spirit they are of." (Luke 9:55.) That ability comes from renewing your mind to the Word of the Lord, from pounding it in day and night, from meditating on it until it permeates and saturates your entire being. Then everything you do will be successful, because you will "know wisdom and instruction" and "perceive the words of understanding."

31

Receiving Instruction—

"To receive the instruction of wisdom,..." (v. 3a). Recalling that the word "instruction" means discipline, verse three tells us what discipline is good for: to receive the discipline of wisdom, justice and judgment, and equity.

Discipline gives us wisdom. Here we have a different Hebrew word for wisdom: *sakal,* meaning intelligence or good sense. Did you know it takes discipline to have good sense? Have you ever met one of those teenagers who had good sense? My friend, that trait did not just fall upon him out of the sky. Good sense is something that has to be disciplined into a child. The ability to make wise choices is not something a person is just born with. Nor is it something he just "lucks into." This kind of wisdom is not a natural gift, it is an acquired habit!

Proverbs 22:15 states: "Foolishness is bound in the heart of a child; but the rod of correction shall drive it far from him." It takes discipline to rid children of foolishness and replace it with good sense. That's why many times the wisest young people we have ever seen are those who have been brought up "in the nurture and admonition of the Lord" (Eph. 6:4). Sometimes the good sense my own children display astounds even me. This is the result of constant exposure to the Word, discipline, and the ways of the Lord.

"...justice,..." (v. 3b). The word translated "justice" here actually refers to the treating of other people as your equals. Did you know that God treats YOU as His equal? He never looks down on you. Never demeans you. Never berates you. God never talks down to His children. Rather He talks to us as His equals. That should be a lesson to us parents. Discipline will teach us to treat our children with dignity and respect, as equals in righteousness.

"...and judgment,..." (v. 3c). Now this has to do with judging things correctly. The Bible tells us that we are never to judge people. (Rom. 2:1-3.) But we ARE to judge THINGS.

(1 Cor. 2:15.) You can love a person and still hate what he does. Jesus did that: He loved sinners and despised sin. He loved the disciples, but rebuked them for their wrong attitudes and actions. So it's not wrong to correct a person for what he does wrong, as long as you still love him while you are doing it.

"...and equity" (v. 3d). "Equity" means evenness, fairness, impartiality. There is a discipline to equity.

For example, it takes discipline to treat all of your children equally. There are times when I might be out somewhere with my son and buy him something. Do you know what happens the minute we get home? He runs to his sister to show her what Daddy bought him. And what do you think she does then? She comes running to me asking what I bought her. Unless I have something for her, she immediately starts in on me to take her out and buy her a gift too. Now I might have a hundred things to do right at that moment, but I have learned to discipline myself to treat my children with equity. So what do I do? I postpone everything long enough to take my daughter to the store to get her something she would like. Why? To show her that her father does not treat her brother better than he does her.

Now in cases like that, there is always the tendency to put it off, to say, "Oh Honey, I'm really busy right now. Can't we do it tomorrow?" She might agree to that, but I try not to do it. Because although she might agree on the outside, on the inside she could be thinking, "Daddy doesn't love me as much as he does Brother." And that possibility is not worth the risk. Therefore, as much as I am able, I practice equity toward my children. I also try to practice it toward all other people, whether I feel like it or not. Equity requires discipline.

Wisdom For All—

"To give subtilty to the simple,..." (v. 4a). The next three verses take up excuses for not acquiring wisdom. Some say

they are too ignorant or too uneducated to understand the Word of God. The word translated "simple" actually means stupid. Did you know the Bible even instructs stupid people? That's really the only reason any of us know what we know. Of ourselves none of us is capable enough to truly understand the deep things of God. They are revealed to us by God's own Spirit. (1 Cor. 2:11.) In Matthew 11:25, Jesus prayed: "I thank thee, O Father, Lord of heaven and earth, because thou hast hid these things from the wise and prudent, and hast revealed them unto babes." And Isaiah tells us that God has made His way so clear that even "the wayfaring men, though fools, shall not err therein" (Is. 35:8). So ignorance is no excuse for a lack of wisdom.

"...to the young man knowledge and discretion" (v. 4b). Another excuse is youth. Well, not according to this verse. Even the young are taught knowledge and discretion by a study of God's Word.

What is discretion? It's the wisdom that keeps a person from future trouble. Now think about this: why would a young man or a young woman need discretion?

It is important that children learn early in life to be discreet, to be wise. Because when so many youngsters (especially church kids) get to be teenagers, they are gullible. They are so innocent and trusting they swallow anything and everything they are told without the least bit of hesitation. They need more discernment than that. They need to learn that not everybody in life is like those folks down at the church.

There is a real world out there run by a very real devil. And the devil is out to kill, steal and destroy. (John 10:10.) Unless children are trained and prepared for what they will encounter in the future, their chances of survival are severely reduced. They need to be taught to recognize evil so they can walk with discretion, being as wise as serpents and as harmless as doves. (Matt. 10:16.)

"A wise man will hear, and will increase learning; and a man of understanding shall attain unto wise counsels" (v. 5). Then there is just the opposite excuse—that the person is so educated or enlightened he doesn't need any more wisdom. Verse five says that a wise man will hear, and will increase his learning. No one ever gets to the place where he knows it all. Even if you are already wise, the Word of God can make you even wiser.

"To understand a proverb, and the interpretation; the words of the wise, and their dark sayings" (v. 6). Here we see that not only must we understand these proverbs, we must also understand their interpretation. A practical application of verses five through seven can be found in three verses of Chapter 9.

Applying Wisdom—

PROVERBS 9:7-9

He that reproveth a scorner getteth to himself shame: and he that rebuketh a wicked man getteth himself a blot.

Reprove not a scorner, lest he hate thee: rebuke a wise man, and he will love thee.

Give instruction to a wise man, and he will be yet wiser: teach a just man, and he will increase in learning.

"He that reproveth a scorner getteth to himself shame..." (v. 7a). This passage tells us who can reprove and who we are not to reprove. There is one person we are never to reprove: a scorner. Sometimes there is a tendency for sinners to mock us Christians and to make fun of us. Solomon would counsel us not to attempt to reprove a scorner. If you try, you will regret it. Chances are, you will only make matters worse. It is very difficult to get the best of a scorner. You will only end up bringing shame on yourself and the cause of Christ.

Even if you succeed in "telling off" a scorner, what have you accomplished? As the saying goes, "What have you *gained* when you've bested a fool?" Certainly not a new convert to the Lord!

Then if we are not to reprove a scorner, how should we react? What are we supposed to do to someone who purposely and maliciously holds us up to public ridicule? Love him. As Jesus taught us in Luke 6:27,28: "But I say unto you, Love your enemies, do good to them which hate you, bless them that curse you, and pray for them which despitefully use you."

"...and he that rebuketh a wicked man getteth himself a blot" (v. 7b). Now who is the "wicked man" in this verse? The wicked man is not just any sinner. This is the person who is caught up entirely in very evil, wicked works—the person who is totally and consciously sold out to the devil. What happens if you try to rebuke such a person? Proverbs says you only get yourself a "blot" on your record. A blot is an accounting term. It refers to God's scorecard. As Christians, we are not sent into all the world to rebuke sinners; we are sent to SAVE sinners. In the game of life, rebuking the people for whom Christ Jesus suffered and died does not win points with the Lord; on the contrary, it only gets you demerits!

"Reprove not a scorner, lest he hate thee..." (v. 8a). If you do reprove a scorner, you will never win Him to Christ. What are we supposed to do instead? Love him. Give a scorner love and he won't know what to do with it. The most confusing thing in the world to a sinner is love. He doesn't understand it. When someone attacks you verbally, don't get even—get ahead! Win your adversary to the Lord and increase his blessing AND yours!

"...rebuke a wise man, and he will love thee" (v. 8b). Here we see the one person we can reprove—the wise man. And what's more, he will love us for it!

"Give instruction to a wise man, and he will be yet wiser: teach a just man, and he will increase in learning" (v. 9). Recalling that instruction means discipline, it is the wise man who will receive reproof. The wiser people are, the more they appreciate being corrected. Why? Because they know that the more they learn, the wiser and happier they become. To him who has, even more will be given. (Matt. 25:29.) That is a spiritual law. The truly wise understand that law and benefit from it.

The world offers us addictives like caffeine, nicotine, alcohol and heroin. God's wisdom is addictive also. The more of it you get, the more you want. That's why the wise love reproof and correction. Because they know it makes them even wiser. And, unlike the world's addictives, God's addictive pays rich dividends—riches, honor and long life!

The Beginning of Knowledge—

"The fear of the Lord is the beginning of knowledge: but fools despise wisdom and instruction" (v. 7). Has someone ever tried to correct you and it made you mad? If so, all you proved was that you don't have the very thing he was trying to give you—wisdom. He thought you were wise, but you proved him wrong.

When someone tries to correct you, don't get mad or try to retaliate. Take time to listen. If he's wrong, all you've lost is a few minutes of your time. If he's right, you have learned something; you're now even smarter than you were.

Do you want to be more knowledgeable, more understanding, more successful? Then read on! And as you read, be wise. Be open to receive reproof and correction if you need it. Some of these scriptures may hurt a bit; some of them just might "strike home." If so, don't become angry or bitter. Allow the Lord to teach you, knowing that the fear of the Lord is the beginning of knowledge. If you accept correction graciously, you will be all the wiser.

In Second Timothy 3:16,17 the Apostle Paul tells us: "All scripture is given by inspiration of God, and is profitable for doctrine, for reproof, for correction, for instruction in righteousness: that the man of God may be perfect (mature), throughly furnished unto all good works." When you have finished your journey through the book of Proverbs, you will be more "throughly furnished," more thoroughly equipped for good works than when you began. Like your Lord (the Divine Author of this book), you will continue to increase in wisdom and stature (knowledge), and in favor with God and man. (Luke 2:52.)

2
The Person of Wisdom
Proverbs 8:22-36; 1:20-33

Many times we look upon wisdom as a thing. But the book of Proverbs sees wisdom as a person; we need to understand that. Sometimes Proverbs will say, "Get wisdom, get understanding"; but other times wisdom itself will speak. Sometimes wisdom will talk for two or three chapters, expressing itself, explaining how it functions, describing what it is looking for, stressing its results, promising what it will do for the one who possesses it.

In Proverbs 8, wisdom identifies itself. See if you can figure out who wisdom is.

Wisdom as the Creator—

PROVERBS 8:22-29

The Lord possessed me in the beginning of his way, before his works of old.

I was set up from everlasting, from the beginning, or ever the earth was.

When there was no depths, I was brought forth; when there were no fountains abounding with water.

Before the mountains were settled, before the hills was I brought forth:

While as yet he had not made the earth, nor the fields, nor the highest part of the dust of the world.

When he prepared the heavens, I was there: when he set a compass upon the face of the depth:

When he established the clouds above: when he strengthened the fountains of the deep:

When he gave to the sea his decree, that the waters should not pass his commandments: when he appointed the fountains of the earth.

Who would you say wisdom is? Wisdom is *Jesus*.

The world is looking for a thing called wisdom. Remember what we read in Job 28? How man looks into the depths, into nature, into the sky, into creation, trying to find wisdom? But wisdom cannot be found by looking at things. In order to locate wisdom, we must go back to the origin of all things—back even past creation—all the way back to the *Creator*. Because wisdom created all things.

"In the beginning was the Word, and the Word was with God, and the Word was God.

"The same was in the beginning with God.

"All things were made by him; and without him was not any thing made that was made" (John 1:1-3).

A few verses later John tells us: "And the Word was made flesh, and dwelt among us, (and we beheld his glory, the glory as of the only begotten of the Father,) full of grace and truth" (John 1:14).

The Word of God is Jesus. He was there at the time of Creation. John says He was with God and He was God and that nothing was created without Him. Paul tells us that this same Jesus has been made unto us wisdom. (1 Cor. 1:30.) Wisdom is not a thing, it is a person. When you and I were born again, when Jesus came into our lives, *wisdom* set up residence within us.

Wisdom is a person! Wisdom is the Lord Jesus Christ. Therefore it is ridiculous to look for wisdom in things, because it was wisdom which created ALL things. The spiritual and intangible created the material and tangible.

The spirit realm created the natural realm. So you cannot find wisdom by looking at the natural realm. You have to go back to the roots of the natural realm. That's where wisdom is found, in the spirit realm. Wisdom is found in the person of the Lord Jesus Christ.

Wisdom as a Woman—

The question arises: Why then does the book of Proverbs portray wisdom as a woman? Simply because that was the only way Solomon knew how to personify what was to him a living entity. Solomon loved women and wanted to convey the idea that, like a woman, wisdom will spurn the one who mistreats her. As with a beautiful woman, you cannot neglect, ignore, abuse or take unfair advantage of wisdom and still enjoy her favor. Wisdom is every bit a lady, but—like God—she is also jealous; she does not look kindly upon unfaithfulness. Nor will she allow herself to be betrayed with impunity. As the old saying has it, "Hell hath no fury like that of a woman scorned." Wisdom is no exception to that rule.

In a marriage relationship, the man was designed to be the aggressive one. It is he who is to woo and win, love and cherish, protect and defend, watch over and provide for his mate. Then she in turn will respond with affection, respect, admiration and appreciation. The Apostle Paul exhorted husbands to love their wives even as Christ also loved the Church and gave Himself for it (Eph. 5:25), concluding with this statement: "...let every one of you in particular (as individuals) so love his wife even as himself; and the wife see that she reverence her husband" (v. 33). In other words, "If you want your wife to love you, love her."

In the same way, Solomon is telling us, "If you want the favor of wisdom, you must favor her. Because, like a woman, she will treat you as you treat her." And with seven hundred wives and three hundred concubines, Solomon ought to know what he is talking about! (Read the Song of

Solomon sometime in a modern translation; Solomon was an expert on love!)

Proverbs compares wisdom to women. It compares God's wisdom, which is symbolized by a virtuous woman, to the wisdom of the world, which is represented by an evil adulteress. Solomon knew about both. He knew what it was like to find a virtuous woman, a good and honest and faithful woman who truly loves her husband and family. He also knew what it was like to live with a beautiful but vain and immoral and unfaithful woman who brings shame and dishonor upon those who love her the most.

Wisdom as the Word—

Proverbs 8 told us that Wisdom is Jesus. But Jesus is also the Word of God. (Rev. 19:13.) John says that the Word became flesh and dwelt among us. So wisdom is not only Jesus Christ, it is also His Word.

Just because you have Jesus doesn't necessarily mean that you automatically manifest wisdom to handle every situation of life. Just because you *have* the mind of Christ doesn't necessarily mean that you have *manifested* the mind of Christ. Yes, your spirit man does have the mind of Christ. The moment you were born again, you received wisdom; but wisdom for the daily affairs of life doesn't need to be in your SPIRIT, it needs to be in your MIND where you can use it. That's why it takes diligence in the Word of God. You've got to appropriate the wisdom that has been made available to you through Jesus Christ.

"Study to shew thyself approved unto God, a workman that needeth not to be ashamed, rightly dividing the word of truth" (2 Tim. 2:15). As you become diligent in the Word, you transfer that Word from your spirit to your mind. And it's the wisdom in your mind that helps you to handle the day-to-day activities of your life. You will still face situations, calamities, distresses, just like everyone else. The difference is that you will have access to wisdom that the world does not know about.

You will recall that the main word for wisdom in the book of Proverbs is *chokmah* which we said had to do with "pounding in" something. Yes, you have wisdom resident in your spirit. But that wisdom will do you no good as long as it remains stored away in your inner man; it must be pounded into your mind by confession, study and meditation day and night. Proverbs 3 says that not only must you receive wisdom, you must also retain it. Wisdom comes through the New Birth, but it is retained through daily study of the Word of God.

If you don't attend to the Word (the wisdom) of God, then don't expect it to be there when you need it. In times of distress, you'll find yourself in the same shape as the sinner, dependent upon your own strength.

Wisdom Rejoices in Us—

VERSES 30-32

Then was I by him, as one brought up with him: and I was daily his delight, rejoicing always before him.

Rejoicing in the habitable part of his earth; and my delights were with the sons of men.

Now therefore hearken unto me, O ye children: for blessed are they that keep my ways.

"...*and I was daily his delight...*" (v. 30b). Notice that the Father rejoices in the Son. But who does the Son rejoice in? The answer is found in the next verse.

"...*and my delights were with the sons of men*" (v. 31b). YOU and I are the delight of the Lord Jesus Christ. The Father delights in Jesus, but Jesus delights in US. So when the earth was created, Jesus didn't rejoice in the trees, or in the animals, He rejoiced in the sons of men.

"...blessed are they that keep my ways" (v. 32b). Notice that it is one thing to know God's ways, but it's another thing to keep them. This verse makes it clear that God's blessings are reserved, not for hearers of the Word, but for doers of the Word. (James 1:22.)

Throughout the Bible we are warned to stay in the Word, to meditate on it, to avoid the way of the sinner, not to sit in the seat of the scornful. There are blessings promised to those who will heed and obey these admonitions. Everything they put their hand to will prosper. Likewise, we are told that those who transgress God's commandments will NOT be blessed. They will not prosper. The choice is left to each believer either to obey and be blessed or to disobey and suffer loss.

What the Lord is trying to tell us is simply this: We cannot neglect His Word and still expect wisdom to be there at our beck and call. In order to reap the blessing of wisdom, we must sow to wisdom. That is spiritual law. Wisdom rejoices in the sons of men. But to benefit from the blessings of wisdom, the sons of men must also rejoice in wisdom.

Wisdom Pays Dividends—

VERSES 33-36

Hear instruction, and be wise, and refuse it not.

Blessed is the man that heareth me, watching daily at my gates, waiting at the posts of my doors.

For whoso findeth me findeth life, and shall obtain favour of the Lord.

But he that sinneth against me wrongeth his own soul: all they that hate me love death.

"For whoso findeth me findeth life, and shall obtain favour of the Lord" (v. 35). Notice that we must seek for wisdom in order to find it. The search for true wisdom is not easy,

it demands time and effort. Wisdom does not come automatically, you have to search for it. But the results of wisdom are well worth all the pain and effort. Because with wisdom comes the favor of God.

Wisdom Cries Out to the Simple—

PROVERBS 1:20-23

Wisdom crieth without; she uttereth her voice in the streets:

She crieth in the chief place of concourse, in the openings of the gates: in the city she uttereth her words, saying,

How long, ye simple ones, will ye love simplicity? and the scorners delight in their scorning, and fools hate knowledge?

Turn you at my reproof: behold, I will pour out my spirit unto you, I will make known my words unto you.

"Wisdom crieth without, she uttereth her voice in the streets" (v. 20). Where does wisdom dwell? Is wisdom confined within the walls of the church building? Is wisdom found only in the Christian home? Is wisdom to be found only in "proper" environments? No. Wisdom cries in the street.

"She crieth in the chief place of concourse, in the openings of the gates; in the city she uttereth her words..." (v. 21). Too often we Christians want to stay "holed up" in the safety and sanctity of our churches and homes. After all, that's where the blessings are supposed to be. We live insulated lives, safe and sound within the four walls of our auditoriums and living rooms (they aren't called "sanctuaries" and "dens" for nothing!). We try to hide out from the real live world; we're afraid we might get "tainted" if we come into too close contact with "this vile world." Yet it was precisely "this vile world" which God so loved that

He gave His only begotten Son to die for it. And it was into "this vile world" that He sent us to proclaim the Good News of that great love and mercy!

My friend, we shouldn't go to church *just to get blessed*; we should go there to get "tanked up" on love and mercy so we can then go out into "this vile world" and spread it! The world *is* vile—that's why it needs US and what we have and know.

Where does wisdom abide? Wisdom abides in the streets. In the marketplaces. In the busy thoroughfares and crowded crossroads. Wisdom abides "without." In Colossians 4:5 Paul admonishes us: "Walk in wisdom toward them that are without..." You see, the sinner is the one who is without. In Ephesians 2:11 Paul reminds us "that at (one) time ye were without Christ, being aliens..., and strangers..., having no hope, and without God in the world." Jesus said: "But go ye and learn what that meaneth, I will have mercy and not sacrifice: for I am not come to call the righteous, but sinners to repentance" (Matt. 9:13). That's why wisdom cries "without"; because that's where she is needed most, that's where the sinners are!

So the best place to witness is where people congregate. It's good to witness one-to-one in private, but it's also good to get right out in the middle of the busy marketplaces of life and proclaim the Word of the Lord. Missionaries often do this in foreign countries—they go where the most people are. That's where wisdom cries out.

"How long, ye simple ones, will ye love simplicity? and the scorners delight in their scorning, and fools hate knowledge?" (v. 22). Notice that there are three types of people listed in this verse. First are the "simple ones." Do you know what "simple" means? It means stupid. Now who are the stupid ones? These are carnal Christians, those who know the way of the Lord but don't follow it. Such people as this go into all the world all right. But not to call sinners to repentance;

they go to join them in their sin. They try to straddle the fence, keeping one foot in the church and the other in the world. It won't work. So they are unhappy. Wisdom calls the simple to commitment.

The next type of people in the street are the "scorners." The scorners are unbelievers who scoff and ridicule what they don't understand. They delight in making fun of both the faith and the faithful. Wisdom calls the scorners to repentance.

Fools are also unbelievers. But unlike scorners, fools don't scoff and ridicule, they just turn their backs on God and His Word. They have no interest in the truth. That's why they are called foolish; they have no idea what it is they are refusing or the consequences of their refusal. Wisdom calls fools to knowledge.

"Turn you at my reproof..." (v. 23a). So wisdom cries out both to the carnal Christian and to the sinner: "Simples ones, turn from your simplicity; scorners, turn from your scorning; fools, turn from your hatred of knowledge."

"...behold, I will pour out my spirit unto you. I will make known my words unto you" (v. 23b). Notice the two things that will happen if these people will turn from their evil ways. First, the Spirit will be given them. Secondly, the Word will be made known to them. A person cannot have the Word until he has first received the Spirit. So the first thing that wisdom does is offer the Spirit which then leads the individual to the Word. Once a person is born again or comes back into fellowship with the Lord, the Spirit of God is given to minister to him the Word of the Lord. (Eph. 5:14.)

Wisdom Mocks the Proud—

VERSES 24-26

Because I have called, and ye have refused; I have stretched out my hand, and no man regarded;

47

But ye have set at nought all my counsel, and would none of my reproof:

I also will laugh at your calamity; I will mock when your fear cometh.

"I also will laugh at your calamity; I will mock when your fear cometh" (v. 26). Notice this word "also." If you have laughed at wisdom, it will one day laugh at you.

Some people stay out of church for months at a time, but the moment they get into trouble they run to the pastor for help. They expect to be able to receive a year's worth of wisdom in only 20 or 30 minutes. They need it immediately! This verse is saying that we cannot count on wisdom unless we have invested the time it takes to develop wisdom.

God's Word is not like an insurance policy. We can't let it lay around in a drawer or on a shelf gathering dust until time of disaster, and then expect to grab it up and "make a claim" on it. It just doesn't work that way. God's wisdom works *for* us to the degree we work *at* it! No more, no less. Wisdom warns us that if we refuse to heed her now, the day will come when calamity will befall us; and then will be her turn to refuse to heed us.

Wisdom Rejects Fools—

VERSES 27-32

When your fear cometh as desolation, and your destruction cometh as a whirlwind; when distress and anguish cometh upon you.

Then shall they call me, but I will not answer; they shall seek me early, but they shall not find me:

For that they hated knowledge, and did not choose the fear of the Lord:

They would none of my counsel: they despised all my reproof.

Therefore shall they eat of the fruit of their own way, and be filled with their own devices.

For the turning away of the simple shall slay them, and the prosperity of fools shall destroy them.

Many Christians ask: "If this prosperity message works so well, then why do the sinners of this world seem to be so much better off than we are? Why does it take so long for the Lord to ever begin to prosper a believer? Seems to me that some other way besides faith would work faster than this!"

Yes, other ways might "work" faster. But it's not how quick you get it, it's how long it lasts! Wisdom is not a "quick fix." The way of the Lord is sometimes painfully slow, but its dividends are well worth the wait.

If you want to be truly prosperous in this life, wait on the Lord. Trust Him. Be patient. Diligence will produce. When it does, you will know how to handle that prosperity properly. Because you will have taken the time to develop in wisdom and knowledge.

"*...the prosperity of fools shall destroy them*" (v. 32b). The world's way is "easy come, easy go." Non-Christians often prosper quickly, but just as often they don't know how to manage what they have acquired, so either they lose it entirely or else it ends up causing them pain and unhappiness. It "destroys" them. But God's way is different.

Wisdom Protects the Wise—

VERSE 33

But whoso hearkeneth unto me shall dwell safely, and shall be quiet from fear of evil.

The Christian faces the same problems and calamities that the world faces. He has the same difficulties and disappointments as the carnal Christian. The difference is that

49

the world and carnal believers do not have the wisdom to handle the trials and tribulations of life. Those who love the Lord and are faithful to Him do have that wisdom. The Word of God keeps them safe and quiet from all fear through the darkest of times. They know how to deal with every situation of life.

When the world doesn't have the answer, the wise man will know just what is to be done. He will emerge victorious from every trying circumstance. Everything he puts his hand to will prosper. In time of famine he will be fed and in time of disaster he will be protected. Because wisdom will be there to guide him in the paths of the Lord.

That wisdom which guides us into all truth and gives us victory in every situation is a person: the Lord Jesus Christ, whom to know is life!

3
Co-Signing
Proverbs 6:1-5; 22:26,27

PROVERBS 6:1,2

My son, if thou be surety for this friend, if thou
hast stricken thy hand with a stranger,

Thou art snared in the words of thy mouth, thou
art taken with the words of thy mouth.

Our first practical lesson from the wisdom of Proverbs
concerns the matter of co-signing.

*"My son, if thou be surety for this friend, if thou hast stricken
thy hand with a stranger"* (v. 1). To "be surety" for someone
is to co-sign with him for a loan.

"Thou art snared with the words of thy mouth..." (v. 2a).
We have quoted this verse (and heard it quoted) quite often,
usually in reference to "confession." This scripture is one
of those used to illustrate the power of the tongue. That
power is very real, and we should give attention to our
speech. However, considering this verse in its context, we
see that it really is not speaking of the creative power of the
tongue at all. Rather it is stressing the need for wisdom and
caution in this matter of co-signing. In these words, Solomon
is emphasizing the fact that when we give our word as surety
for another person—whether friend or stranger—we are
making ourselves liable for that person's debt.

Dangers of Co-Signing—

PROVERBS 22:26,27

Be not thou one of them that strike hands, or of
them that are sureties for debts.

If thou hast nothing to pay, why should he take away the bed from under thee?

"Be thou not one of them that...are sureties for debts" (v. 26). This verse states that we are not to co-sign for the debt of another person. It does not say that co-signing is necessarily a sin, but it does make it quite clear that it is not a wise practice. Why? What's wrong with helping out a close friend by going in with him to guarantee his loan?

Let's think about that for a minute. Suppose I come across a great deal on a limited edition automobile that I just know will one day be a classic and return at least two or three times the amount of my investment. But suppose also that I don't have a strong enough credit record to finance such an expensive car on my own. But I have a good friend named George who is quite well off. I'm sure "ole buddy George" will agree to co-sign with me for a loan. So I rush over to see my friend to try to persuade him to go in with me on the deal. What's wrong with that?

Seemingly nothing. That's what friends are for, right? But let's just suppose that the reason George is so prosperous is because he is wise in the Word of God. His wealth has not come to him because of his natural business ability, but as a result of the financial wisdom God has given him. What will George's response likely be?

"Bob," he says, putting his arm around me, "you and I are the very best of friends. So let me level with you. I hope you won't take this wrong, I'd be glad to help you out any way I can. But in all honesty, Bob, you are asking me to do something I just can't agree to. The Word says that it is not wise to co-sign with anyone. Being a man of God, I'm sure you understand, don't you?"

If I were to get mad because George wouldn't co-sign with me on that deal, who would be in error—George or me? Obviously I would. And if I broke off my friendship with George over it, whose fault would that be—his or mine?

Mine, of course. But besides that, not only would it be my fault, it would prove two things: 1) My own lack of character, and 2) the fact that I never was a real friend to George in the first place.

Like George, never feel obligated to guarantee someone else's debt. And certainly you should never co-sign with someone simply because you are afraid you might offend them or endanger your "friendship" if you refuse. Remember: If your supposed friendship depends on your co-signing against your will, that relationship was on mighty shaky ground to begin with. You risk nothing when you risk losing a "friend" like that. Because a true friend would never put you on the spot or try to make you feel obliged to do something against your convictions or your better judgment.

Co-signing is dangerous, even with the best of friends. More friends have been separated by money than just about any other thing in the world. If George agreed to co-sign with me—even if everything seemed fine, even if our friendship was strong and I was the most honest man on earth—there would still be a danger involved.

Suppose, for example, that after co-signing for that note, something happened to me so I could no longer work. Suppose some member of my family was hospitalized for a long period of time at tremendous expense to me. Suppose I just honestly could not make the payments on that note. Who would then be responsible for them? George. If I fell behind in my payments, before the finance company came to repossess the car, they would contact George to collect what was overdue. That alone is enough to put an unnecessary strain on our friendship, especially if it goes on for any length of time. Volunteering to help out a friend financially in time of crisis is one thing, but being *forced* to pay someone else's bills can get old in a hurry!

"If thou hast nothing to pay, why should he take away the bed from under thee?" (v. 27). What would happen if I defaulted

on my loan and the repossessed car didn't sell for enough to cover the outstanding debt? As co-signer of the note, George would be liable for the difference, wouldn't he? But suppose George didn't have the ready cash at the time to cover that debt? Suppose he had his liquid assets tied up in investments, or out on loan, or committed to other long-term projects? George would not be too happy to come home one day and discover that his furniture had been seized to pay off the unpaid balance. He would be even less thrilled at having his income garnisheed. And what do you think his feelings toward me, his best friend, would be if my "ole buddy George" found himself slapped with a lawsuit for failure to make good on *my* debt?

What would your feelings be in a situation like that? Then don't run that risk. Don't co-sign for other people!

Proverbs 17:18 says: "A man void of understanding striketh hands, becometh surety in the presence of his friend." Co-signing is not a wise practice. Solomon says that it shows a lack of understanding.

"He that is surety for a stranger shall smart for it: and he that hateth surety is sure" (Prov. 11:15). The first part of this verse does not mean to say that it is smart to co-sign, just the opposite; it means that the person who does so will end up *suffering* (smarting) for it. If you are wise, you will refrain from co-signing. Refusing to co-sign for a friend is not selfish; the Bible says it is wisdom.

Escape from Co-signing—

But what if you have already co-signed with someone? Let's look at Proverbs 6:1,2 again:

"My son, if thou be surety for this friend, if thou hast stricken thy hand with a stranger,

"Thou art snared with the words of thy mouth, thou art taken with the words of thy mouth."

Notice the two words, "snared" and "taken." They mean two different things. What this passage is saying is that surety is like a trap that is laid for an animal. When he steps into it, he is snared or caught. Then once he is caught, he is taken or dragged away. If you have assumed responsibility for the debts of someone else (a friend or a stranger), either with the words of your mouth or with a handshake, you are snared, you are trapped. You will soon be taken, dragged away. You need to get out of that situation as quickly as possible. But how? What can you do once you have been trapped by the words of your mouth?

VERSES 3-5

Do this now, my son, and deliver thyself, when thou art come into the hand of thy friend; go, humble thyself, and make sure thy friend.

Give not sleep to thine eyes, nor slumber to thine eyelids.

Deliver thyself as a roe from the hand of the hunter, and as a bird from the hand of the fowler.

"Do this NOW, my son,..." (v. 3a). Do this when? NOW. That doesn't mean get ready to do it now, it means to DO it now, right this minute. Do what?

"...deliver thyself,..." (v. 3b). DELIVER YOURSELF from that situation. Don't wait on someone else to get you out, get busy extricating yourself from that bondage. But how do you go about that?

"...Go, humble thyself, and make sure thy friend" (v. 3c). Make your friendship secure. Keep in close contact with that friend. Don't let him out of your sight. Keep your relationship as solid as you can. See to it, as the Irish say, that "the hinges of your friendship never get rusty!"

"Give not sleep to thine eyes, nor slumber to thine eyelids" (v. 4). Don't give yourself any rest until you have done

everything in your power to assure that your friend keeps his part of the bargain. Be right there to make sure that nothing goes wrong.

"Deliver thyself as a roe from the hand of the hunter, and as a bird from the hand of the fowler". A roe is a deer or a gazelle. When does a trapped animal begin to try to free itself? NOW! So make certain that the person with whom you co-signed remains your friend. Don't give him any excuse to cause you trouble. Watch for an opportunity to free yourself from that entanglement. Once you are free, learn a lesson from that experience: Never allow yourself to get into that predicament again!

Acceptable Co-Signing—

"My breath is corrupt, my days are extinct, the graves are ready for me.

"Are there not mockers with me? and doth not mine eye continue in their provocation?

"Lay down now, put me in a surety with thee; who is he that will strike hands with me?" (Job. 17:1-3).

"My breath is corrupt..." (v. 1a). "Breath" here refers to the spirit, the inner man. In this passage Job realizes what a sinner (debtor) he is. He becomes aware of his backslidden (bankrupt) condition. He is in great desperation (debt). He is corrupt (penniless), without hope of redeeming himself from his mockers (creditors).

"Lay down now, put me in a surety with thee; who is he that will strike hands with me" (v. 3). My friend, when a person is lost, he is corrupt. No matter how much he thinks he can do, or how strong he imagines himself to be, regardless of his supposed great intellect or capability, he cannot pay the fine for his sins. He is bankrupt. Sooner or later he must come to grips with himself and his helpless condition. He will have to acknowledge his own inability to save himself.

That's when he will realize, like Job, that he desperately needs someone to "co-sign" for him, someone to agree to pay his unpayable debt FOR him. That is his only hope.

If you are a Christian, you were once in that very same situation, remember? You woke up one day and realized that you were bankrupt, in debt with no hope of redeeming yourself. You desperately needed someone to be "surety" for you. And then you heard of a Friend who had already paid your debt for you by the sacrifice of His own life. Wasn't that good news!

"By so much was Jesus made a *surety* of a better testament" (Heb. 7:22). There was a time when I was as bankrupt as you were. How I wished there was someone who would just co-sign for me, someone who would shake hands with me and agree to pay my debt. Then the greatest Hand of all time reached down from heaven and took hold of mine. At that moment I met the Lord Jesus Christ—my Redeemer—for the very first time. He took my debt and paid it in full. Then, in exchange, He gave me His riches. What a deal! What a Friend!

4
The Sluggard
Proverbs 6:6-11; 24:30-34; 26:13-20

The book of Proverbs is full of very practical wisdom that is meant to be applied to our everyday lives to make us happier and more successful. However, that wisdom is not always expressed in the most polite or tactful manner. When wisdom speaks, sometimes she can be very blunt!

In fact, sometimes wisdom fairly "slaps us in the face." But when she does that, it is always for a purpose—to shake us awake, to cause us to open our eyes and see the danger that is creeping up on us while we sleep. As hard and unfeeling as wisdom may seem at times, she always has our best interest at heart. She is trying to save us from some pending disaster or future loss. If we will only heed her warnings and counsel, wisdom will give us tremendous insight into human nature—our nature as well as that of others.

Although we like for things to be sweet and nice, unfortunately in this world in which we live that is not always the case. In order to survive, we must learn to deal with people and their attitudes and actions. Some of those attitudes and actions are just not very pleasant. And for a good reason. You see, we have an enemy out there named Satan. Now he doesn't manifest himself as he is so often pictured in cartoons; the devil doesn't wear red tights and carry a pitchfork. (It would be better for us if he did; we could recognize him a lot easier that way!) No, Satan usually manifests himself through people. And we must remember that Christians (even you and I!) are also people.

People can be a means of blessing or of cursing. When God pours out His blessing upon us, it usually comes through human agents. God ministers through the mouths and hands and feet of His people. Our bodies are His instruments.

In the same way, God's enemy Satan manifests himself through human instruments. He works through people. Even Christian people. Even you and me, if we're not careful! If we are not on our guard, the devil will have the very children of God doing his dirty work! That's why it is so important for us to be aware of the devil's tactics. Paul warns us not to be ignorant of Satan's devices. (2 Cor. 2:11.) That's one of the purposes of this study, to instruct us in the ways of the enemy and of those he uses to carry out his diabolical plans. Just as a good football team will study films of their opponents to prepare the best defense and offense to use against them on the playing field, so must we Christians study our opponent and his strategy and tactics in order to overcome him. The Word of God familiarizes us with Satan and warns us about the traps he lays for us. One of those traps we will consider in this chapter.

Go to the Ant—

PROVERBS 6:6-11

Go to the ant, thou sluggard; consider her ways, and be wise:

Which having no guide, overseer, or ruler,

Provideth her meat in the summer, and gathereth food in the harvest.

How long wilt thou sleep, O sluggard? when wilt thou arise out of thy sleep?

Yet a little sleep, a little slumber, a little folding of the hands to sleep:

So shall thy poverty come as one that travelleth, and thy want as an armed man.

"Go to the ant, thou sluggard..." (v. 6a). What is a sluggard? Well, let's define it this way. Do you like to "lie in bed to all hours of the morning"? If so, then you're a sluggard! A sluggard is simply a person who is lazy.

Why should the lazy person "go to" the ant? This expression means to look to, or to consider. What Solomon is telling us here is that God has designed His wisdom in the things of nature. We are literally surrounded with evidences of the wisdom of God. Even if we didn't have the Bible, we could still learn about God through His creation. In his letter to the Romans, Paul says that the invisible things of God can be clearly understood by considering the visible things He has created. (Rom. 1:19,20.) We have said that man cannot find wisdom IN nature, and that is true. But he can find wisdom THROUGH nature, by recognizing the existence and power of God expressed in His creation. But why should we consider the ant in particular? Because the ant is an example of wisdom.

"Which having no guide, overseer, or ruler" (v. 8). The word translated "guide" here is a Hebrew word meaning *commander*. In this sense, the ant is a *type* of the born-again, Spirit-filled believer. Such a person doesn't always need an outside source of guidance. He is guided from the inside.

"Provideth her meat in the summer, and gathereth food in the harvest" (v. 9). Ants instinctively know what to do. They know when to sow, when to reap, when to store up, when to protect themselves. So should Christians. There may be times when a believer will need counsel, but there is a difference between a counselor and a crutch. Counsel was never meant to become a substitute for wisdom, maturity and common sense. True counsel is from the Lord. Most of the time it should be sought by the individual believer himself directly from the Word of God.

Total dependency on one person is crippling, not empowering. Ministers who teach shepherding are crippling their sheep. Their people are not learning to follow their own recreated spirits. Ministers should feed their flock on the Word of God so that when they are out on their own that counsel will remain with them on the inside, leading and guiding them.

As a Christian, you don't always need an outside overseer or ruler. The Word of God is your inward guide. After all, the Word declares that the Lord will never leave you nor forsake you. He will always be there; counselors won't.

"How long wilt thou sleep, O sluggard? when wilt thou arise out of thy sleep? Yet a little sleep, a little slumber, a little folding of the hands to sleep" (vv. 9,10). In this passage, the writer begins to warn against drowsiness. Verse 10 is actually a little poem. "Yet a little sleep" means just a little MORE sleep. I'm sure you've been awakened in the morning by the alarm and reached over and turned it off so you could get "just a few more minutes of sleep." This verse is a warning not to do that—to be diligent instead. When it's time to get up, get up! Don't let a little sleep rob you of your prosperity!

This is very wise counsel. Your practical life is a direct reflection of your spiritual condition. We've studied the laws of prosperity, but here is a practical application of those laws. God will not drop prosperity on you while you lie in bed! It just doesn't happen that way. No matter how much you may give in tithes and offerings, no matter how much faith you may have, no matter how many times you may confess all the prosperity scriptures, you will never experience true and lasting prosperity if you are a lazy Christian!

In 2 Thessalonians 3:10 Paul specifies that if a man doesn't work then he shouldn't be allowed to eat. In 1 Timothy 5:8 he goes on to say that if any man does not provide for his own family, he has denied the faith and is worse than an infidel. Now that's strong language!

In John 5:17 Jesus said, "My Father worketh hitherto, and I work." Many Christians make the mistake of thinking that because they pray and believe and confess, then they're "spiritual." That's not necessarily so. True spirituality comes from being full of the Spirit (or nature) of God. And laziness is NOT part of the nature of God! "My meat is to do the will of him that sent me, and to finish *his* work" Jesus said in John 4:34. God works! So must we.

Luke tells us that the return on our giving will come to us through the hands of *men.* "Through the hands of men" could mean getting a job. I have actually heard people testify, "I've been believing God to meet my financial need, and all I get are job offers!" How do these people think God is going to answer their prayer, by dropping dollar bills on them out of heaven? God's not going to do that. He doesn't have any dollars in heaven to drop. After all, God is not a counterfeiter.

If we want God to do His part to prosper us, then we must do our part. Our part is to work.

"So shall thy poverty come as one that travelleth, and thy want as an armed man" (v. 11.) Just as surely as diligence produces prosperity and abundance, so laziness produces poverty and want. Solomon says poverty will come upon the lazy person "as one that travelleth." What does he mean by that statement? He means it will come like a man walking—one step at a time. In fact, it usually creeps in so slowly and quietly the person is not even aware of what is taking place. Little by little, he finds himself getting farther and farther behind in his payments. He just doesn't seem to be able to "make ends meet" any more. Poverty creeps in slowly, but once it has fully settled in, it is like an armed burglar who has sneaked in and disarmed the householder. There is no more defense against it. It will rob the person of everything he owns.

That's why we are warned to arise out of our slumber. We must be on our guard against "creeping poverty"!

Signs of Laziness—

Lazy people are people who have not studied the lesson to be learned from the ant. They are so given to sleep they allow poverty to overtake them a little at a time.

No one really likes people who are lazy. Especially employers. Every year businessmen lose hundreds of thousands of dollars and untold amounts of valuable time simply because of lazy workers. They spend fortunes hiring management consultants to analyze their companies in an effort to discover how to motivate their employees to turn out more and better products. Psychologists and psychiatrists are brought in to study each individual worker to determine what each one is like and what "makes him tick." The whole business and industrial world is puzzled, they can't understand why their people don't take more pride and interest in their work. They could have saved their money; the answer is right in front of them—for free! The Word of God is full of good business sense. It has the solutions to many of the problems which plague our society today. One of those problems is how to locate and identify sluggards, those who are lazy on the job.

Proverbs describes the tendencies of the lazy. The lazy man just doesn't *want* to work. As a result, he avoids it whenever possible. That's why lazy people never rise very high in positions of authority.

Proverbs 12:24 says, "The hand of the diligent shall bear rule: but the slothful shall be under tribute." The Hebrew word translated "tribute" here is *mic* which *Strong's Exhaustive Concordance* defines as "a *tax* in the form of forced *labor*." A lazy person will never end up being the boss. He'll always be the lowest man on the job scale. It's the diligent man who always rises to the top. Because not only is he diligent in natural practices, he is also diligent in spiritual things as well.

Some people are spiritually lazy. They want to just come to church on Sunday and be spoon-fed. They may come on

Wednesday night, if it doesn't interrupt their schedule. As Christians, we need to rise up and shake ourselves. We need to get our priorities in order. A lazy person has no priorities. He never plans out his day. He just takes the course of least resistance, bouncing from one thing to the other. That's why he is never trusted with authority.

Look at Proverbs 10:26: "As vinegar to the teeth, and as smoke to the eyes, so is the sluggard to them that send him." Lazy people are always an irritation to those around them. They irritate their superiors, the other employees, their parents, their neighbors. Can you think of anything more irritating to your eyes than smoke? Or anything that would set your teeth on edge more than vinegar? Well, there is one thing—a sluggard. When you send him to run an errand or do a job, you'll end up irritated every time because he'll never get it done right.

Lazy people always have the very best of intentions. They are always going to do something big—tomorrow. But never today. They have big ideas, but they never seem to put those ideas into practice. If they do start some project, they never see it through to completion.

Proverbs 12:27 pictures the sluggard this way: "The slothful man roasteth not that which he took in hunting; but the substance of a diligent man is precious." This shows us something else about lazy people: they never appreciate what they have. If you give a sluggard something of value, he will either tear it up, lose it, or let it be destroyed through negligence. He's just too lazy to take care of what little he does have. That's why he doesn't have anything worth owning.

Have you ever lived in the same neighborhood with a sluggard? It wasn't hard to tell what kind of a person lived there, was it? More than likely his yard always needed mowing, his house needed painting, his roof leaked, and his old filthy car was either broken down, leaking oil, or up on blocks. Right? But yet he was always saying, "Y'know, one of these days, I'm really gonna fix this place up. Jus' soon as I git to feelin' better. I been down in my back, y'know." Two years later he's still singing the same tune. He's got the same plans he had two years ago. But he's also still got that "bad back." His problem isn't his back, it's laziness!

When a person works to acquire something, he usually appreciates it a lot more than when it is just given to him. This verse tells us that the lazy man is always looking for a handout, something for nothing. But then when he does get what he wanted, he really doesn't appreciate it because it required no effort on his part.

Proverbs 21:25 says: "The desire of the slothful killeth him; for his hands refuse to labour." The sluggard has great desires, but he never gets anything accomplished. He has all these great intentions on the inside, but he just can't motivate the outside to get up and get going. He's convinced there "oughta be an easier way." This type person is always looking to "get rich quick"; always going to land some big job or close some big business deal "next week." But somehow "next week" never gets here.

We have all heard about those big-paying jobs that don't require much work. But of course, they are always "out of state." If that's what you've been looking for, forget it. You'll never find it. Because, like the sluggard, you're just looking for the pot of gold at the end of the rainbow.

In this life, there is only one tried and true, proven way to prosperity.

It is the way of diligence. Even a gold mine has to be worked before it will produce riches. Prosperity requires effort. It's the *diligent* man who ultimately prospers, who ends up in a position of power and leadership. Because he's the one that both man and God know they can trust with authority, knowing it will be discharged with diligence.

Results of Laziness—

PROVERBS 24:30-34

I went by the field of the slothful, and by the vineyard of the man void of understanding;

And lo, it was all grown over with thorns, and nettles had covered the face thereof, and the stone wall thereof was broken down.

Then I saw, and considered it well; I looked upon it, and received instruction.

Yet a little sleep, a little slumber, a little folding of the hands to sleep;

So shall thy poverty come as one that travelleth; and thy want as an armed man.

"Yet a little sleep...so shall thy poverty come..." (vv. 33-34). This passage illustrates the results of laziness. Notice that the last two verses are identical to Proverbs 6:10,11. This may have been an established proverb from even before Solomon's time which he twice quoted to emphasize the result of placing too much interest on sleep. Or he may have liked what he said so much he repeated it here simply to reinforce his message that too much sleep robs one of his prosperity. In any case, the point is abundantly clear: "If you want to prosper in life, you can't afford to be self-indulgent."

It is easy to allow ourselves to fall for self-indulgence. After all, whose business is it if we want to "grab just a few more winks of shut-eye"? Who's going to be harmed if we sleep "just a teeny bit longer"? The answer of course is obvious. It's OUR business, and WE are the ones who will suffer the consequences of our self-indulgence.

"But what's so wrong with sleeping in just a bit? A little extra sleep never hurt anybody."

The problem is not the sleep, it's the practice. It becomes habit-forming. It becomes a habit which is hard to break. If we're not careful, we will end up going through our whole day just waiting to get back to that "sack."

Besides that, it gives a dangerous and unnecessary toe-hold to the devil who will use it to trip us up if he can. As Christians, we need to be more self-disciplined than that.

Finally, it's wasteful. Christians are to be good stewards of all of God's blessings, including the blessing of time. Benjamin Franklin had a saying, "Dost thou love life? Then do not squander time, for that is the stuff life is made of!" When that alarm goes off, we need to get up and get started on our morning routine. Successful people get an early start on each day, and once they're up they don't go back to bed!

We Christians ought to have it even easier. When we get up in the morning, we can begin by praising God and thus set the tone of the entire day. While the natural man has to rely on his own natural tendencies, the Christian can get up depending on the Spirit of the Lord to help him. The Holy Spirit operates through as as we put the natural things of life into operation. We need to learn to be self-starters, we ought to be able to motivate ourselves. Smith Wigglesworth used to say, "If the Spirit doesn't move me, I move the Spirit!" David had something of the same idea. In Psalm 103:1 he wrote, "Bless the Lord, O my soul..." What he meant was, if there was no encouragement, he would encourage himself. And his words in Psalm 34:1 amplify that thought: "I will bless the Lord at all times: his praise shall continually be in my mouth."

"I went by the field of the slothful,...and lo, it was all grown over with thorns..." (vv. 30-31). So what happens to the sluggard? According to this passage, he ends up in poverty. He sleeps while everything around him grows up in weeds. His whole life revolves around when he can get back to that bed and relax. Remember that the lazy person has the best of

intentions. He'll always tell you what all he *plans* to do. He's very impressive, in fact, with his plans. But those plans never materialize. Because he's too lazy to put them into practice.

Look at Proverbs 13:4: "The soul of the sluggard desireth, and hath nothing; but the soul of the diligent shall be made fat." Both men desire, but only one receives his desire. Why? The difference between the sluggard and the diligent man is simply this: One man puts action to his desire. He is diligent enough to get up from his prayers and begin to put hands and feet to them! Good desires are wonderful, but diligence is the thing that will cause those desires to become reality. James tells us that faith without works is dead. (James 2:17.) Faith must be accompanied by corresponding actions if it is to move any mountains.

Don't be a sluggard spiritually. Don't be a slothful person in the natural either. Shake yourself. Wake yourself up. Put yourself in diligence to the Word of God. The result of laziness is poverty; but the result of diligence is abundance!

The Way of Laziness—

"The way of the slothful man is an hedge of thorns: but the way of the righteous is made plain." The word "slothful" has basically the same meaning as sluggard. "Way" means *path*. Can you walk on a path of thorns? No, you will continually step from one "prick" to another. In the same way, the sluggard goes from one crisis to another. His whole life is one long series of crises and catastrophes. Everything is sharp and prickly to him. In other words, the sluggard hates responsibility. Every time he faces it, he shies away from it. So he is constantly changing his course.

One thing you will find about slothful people is that they have usually had many jobs in their lifetime. They have probably been laid off or fired repeatedly. Yet to them it was never their fault. The sluggard will tell you that each failure was someone else's fault, never his own. Either his boss didn't "understand" him or the work was "beneath" him or some other equally nebulous and evasive answer. A sluggard has difficulty facing reality. Especially the truth of his own shortcomings.

Lazy people have a pride problem. They are conceited. Their real problem is themselves. They never take the blame for their troubles.

If these symptoms describe you and your situation, it would be well for you to examine yourself honestly to see if the root cause of your problem is not your own ego. If it is, then you need to acknowledge that the things that have happened to you in your life are not the fault of the system or your parents or society or other people. They are actually not even the devil's fault. They are your fault. You brought all these troubles upon yourself by your selfish and immature attitude. *You* allowed Satan to take advantage of your weakness. The first step to overcoming a spirit of laziness is to quit blaming your problems on your mate or your employer or the world or the devil; instead, admit to the truth, as difficult as that may be. The truth is that your situation is *your* fault.

Proverbs 18:9 says, "He also that is slothful in his work is brother to him that is a great waster." Notice this word "great." Slothfulness is extremely wasteful. If you have a slothful person working for you, although you may be trying to cut back on expenses and increase your cost efficiency, one sluggard will ruin everything. All your diligence and efficiency in every other department will be destroyed by that one wasteful individual. One sluggard ruins things for everyone. That's his way.

If that person has been you, it's time to face up to that fact and do something about it. The hardest part is admitting your own responsibility for the state of your life. Once you have come to terms with the truth and are able to accept responsibility for your own past actions, then it becomes much easier to accept responsibility for taking positive steps to change those actions. It won't be easy, of course. It will take time and a great deal of effort on your part. No matter how lazy or irresponsible you have been in the past, you *can* overcome laziness. Remember: What is impossible with man is possible with God. (Luke 18:27.) With the help of the Lord, a sluggard can change his ways. If not, there would have been no reason for Solomon to have written the book of Proverbs.

Excuses for Laziness—

PROVERBS 26:13-15

The slothful man saith, There is a lion in the way; a lion is in the streets.

As the door turneth upon his hinges, so doth the slothful upon his bed.

The slothful hideth his hand in his bosom; it grieveth him to bring it again to his mouth.

Proverbs 20:4 says, "The sluggard will not plow by *reason* of the cold; therefore shall he beg in harvest and have nothing." Lazy people always have a "reason" for not working. They can always give some good excuse for their laziness.

"The slothful man saith, There is a lion in the way; a lion is in the streets" (v. 13). Sometimes lazy people go to great extremes for excuses. While lions did occasionally wander into the cities of the ancient world, it was quite uncommon. Yet the mere possibility of danger (however remote) is enough to give a lazy man all the excuse he needs to shirk his responsibility: "I would have been to work on time but there was a lion at my front door. There was a wreck on the freeway and traffic was blocked for miles. My mother had a heart attack." With the sluggard, the exception is the rule. What might happen to anyone else in a year happens to him

every day. His EXCUSES are designed to make you feel guilty for even asking about his lack of attention to his work. I am reminded of the Christian who was so afraid of violating the Lord's Day that he not only wouldn't work on Sunday, he wouldn't work for three days *before* or *after* it! That man was extremely slothful!

"*As the door turneth upon his hinges, so doth the slothful upon his bed*" (v. 14). While it is true that opening a door on its hinges causes the door to move, it really doesn't go anywhere. It doesn't move from place to place. It doesn't travel any distance or accomplish any real work. That is a perfect description of a lazy man. His whole life revolves around his bed. He lives his entire life loving to get in bed and hating to get out.

Because the lazy man is afraid he might have to expend some energy, he never has any. He is always "conserving his strength," which means that he soon loses what strength he does have. We all know that proper exercise doesn't reduce strength, it builds it. The more we use our muscles the more developed they become. By the same token, the less we use our muscles, the weaker they become. We have all seen what happens when a person is confined to a wheelchair for a long period of time. After a while, his arms and chest become strong and muscular from having to wheel himself about, while his legs begin to wither from lack of exercise. That's what happens to the sluggard's strength and energy. What begins as an excuse for avoiding work has a nasty habit of becoming reality. Eventually the lazy man ends up becoming as weak and helpless as he claimed he was!

So a lazy person is really his own worst enemy. His appearance soon reflects his laziness and carelessness. His dress becomes sloppy. His house and yard get run down and overgrown. Inside is a disaster area; it looks like a tornado hit it. His neglected checking account gets hopelessly out of balance. His family life falls apart before his very eyes. Yet the worse things get, the harder it becomes to motivate himself to do anything about them. All these things become like a giant wave washing over him and threatening to destroy him totally. He feels smothered by circumstances, but is too paralyzed by inactivity to do anything but complain and bewail his terrible "fate." That's why he makes excuses for himself, to try to explain away his guilt for shirking his responsibilities.

"The slothful hideth his hand in his bosom; it grieveth him to bring it again to his mouth" (v. 15). Never envy a lazy person. His life is not the carefree existence it may appear on the outside. Because laziness begets laziness. Like that of an alcoholic, the life of a lazy person is a terrible downward spiral which eventually leads to total collapse of all self-esteem. To the slothful person, even the necessary things of life are grievous. The sluggard ends up so listless he has no desire even to eat; it becomes a monumental task to him to have to feed himself. In the final stages of slothfulness, a sluggard is as repulsive as a drunk in the gutter.

The Cause of Laziness—

VERSES 16-19

The sluggard is wiser in his own conceit than seven men that can render a reason.

He that passeth by, and meddleth with strife belonging not to him, is like one that taketh a dog by the ears.

As a mad man who casteth firebrands, arrows, and death.

So is the man that deceiveth his neighbour, and saith, Am I not in sport?

"The sluggard is wiser in his own conceit than seven men that can render a reason" (v. 16). This verse reveals the root problem of sluggards: they are conceited. Conceit is having your eyes on yourself, never considering the rights or feelings

of other people. In his own eyes a sluggard knows more than any seven "lesser" men. A sluggard is *never* wrong; he can always justify himself.

A sluggard has all the answers. Although he won't do his own job, that doesn't stop him from telling everybody else how to do theirs. He knows more about your job than you do, and is not shy about letting you know it. He's always hanging around to tell you what you're doing wrong and what you "shoulda done."

"He that passeth by, and meddleth with strife belonging not to him, is like one that taketh a dog by the ears" (v. 17). A sluggard is always stirring up strife. Taking a dog by the ears is asking for trouble—inevitably you will get bit. Lazy people have usually been fired many times because they would not do their own job. Instead of working, they spent most of their time telling other people how to do their job. Eventually they made the dog mad. They held onto his ears too long. Lazy people have teeth marks all over them. They are covered with scars from the jobs they have lost, the fights they have provoked, the ceilings they have brought down on their own heads. Yet they never seem to learn. Watch out for people like that.

"As a mad man who casteth firebrands, arrows, and death" (v. 18). A lazy person is like a madman with a dangerous weapon, like a crazed sniper who randomly shoots at innocent people from a tall building. But the weapons of the sluggard are not literal firearms. His "firebrands" are words. He goes around sowing dissension, provoking arguments, spreading rumors and stirring up strife—anything to keep from facing the truth of his responsibility for his own misery. He has no control over his own tongue.

"So is the man that deceiveth his neighbour, and saith, Am I not in sport" (v. 19). Lazy people are often practical jokers. If you like practical jokes, be careful. It doesn't take much for that kind of behavior to get out of hand. People don't

really appreciate a practical joker, not for long. A person who has to constantly keep something stirred up is not very stable emotionally. Many times his "jokes" are evidence of a deeper problem, perhaps latent hostility which he disguises as "harmless fun." Sometimes the problem is jealousy or envy. The lazy person does not like to see close friendships develop because he feels left out. If a co-worker has a good working relationship with the boss, the sluggard will try to destroy it out of jealousy. Other times his jokes may be a way of seeking attention; if he can't get it by positive means, he resorts to pranks.

Lazy people are loners. Because of their attitude and behavior they don't have close friends. As a result, they may try to break up other friendships. Backbiting and gossip are favorite ploys of the slothful. They operate under the guise of "concern," but really they are out to tear down rather than to build up.

The longer you are around such a person as this, the more you begin to doubt your own sanity. You begin to think like them. You start to wonder if maybe everybody you thought was for you is really out to get you. You begin to have doubts about yourself and even your closest and dearest friends, perhaps even your mate. What's happening? You are being influenced by the spirit of strife and discord being sowed by the sluggard you're associating with. He is using the words of his mouth to poison your mind, to turn you against those closest to you.

When confronted with wrongdoing, the sluggard will make the excuse that he is "just joking." He claims he really doesn't mean all the things he is saying to you or about you. It's all just a big joke, it was all meant in "sport." Proverbs warns us about this behavior. Don't fall for it.

Usually a practical joker is under self-condemnation and is using his jokes to try to divert attention from the fact that he is not doing his job. He tries to cover up his poor work performance by drawing attention to his "wit" and "humor." Beware of practical jokes and jokers. Often the root cause of their behavior is laziness and conceit.

The Cure for Laziness—

VERSE 20

Where no wood is, there the fire goeth out; so where there is no talebearer, the strife ceaseth.

Although we are supposed to pray for people who cause strife and division, although we are to be patient with them and understand them, many times the best and only thing we can do is to get rid of them; otherwise they will end up ruining our relationships and destroying our work. In Romans 16:17 Paul wrote: "Now I beseech you, brethren, mark them which cause divisions and offences contrary to the doctrine which ye have learned; and avoid them." Sometimes the only thing we can do is to separate ourselves from such people. Do we stop loving them? No. Do we cease praying for them? No. But we have to act in the best interest of ALL concerned. And sometimes that means sending people on their way. As long as they stay around they will go on causing division and being a hindrance to our efforts; to allow them to stay on just causes unnecessary problems for those who are honestly trying to accomplish something worthwhile.

Confusion always accompanies strife: "For where envying and strife is, there is confusion and every evil work" (James 3:16). Confusion is contagious. The real purpose of the strife caused by lazy people is the separation of friends. Proverbs 16:28 says, "A froward man soweth strife: and a whisperer separateth chief (best) friends." The purpose of whispering, slandering, and strife is to separate friendships. Since the lazy man doesn't have any friends of his own, it is easier and more satisfying to break up friendships than to try to form or develop his own. He is jealous of those who do have close friends, so he stirs up strife with his words.

The reason we are studying this subject in such detail is so we can learn to identify this type person and the kind of problems he causes. That is the first step in guarding ourselves against the devices Satan uses to destroy our homes, schools, churches and businesses. I don't mean to point an accusing finger at you or anyone else. However, it is high time we Christians learned to recognize and take a stand against the devil and his unwitting tools. We must especially be sure that WE are not allowing OURSELVES to be used by Satan to destroy lives and hinder the spread of the Gospel. When something goes wrong, one of the surest signs of Christian maturity is the ability to honestly ask ourself, "Was I the cause of that situation? Did I contribute to it?" If the answer is yes, then steps need to be taken to right the situation and to assure that it not happen again.

In Matthew 7:1 our Lord Jesus commanded us, "Judge not, that ye be not judged..." There is only one person we are allowed to judge, and that is our own self. In 2 Corinthians 13:5 Paul writes: "Examine *yourselves*, whether ye be in the faith; prove *your own selves*..." We are not to judge others. We are to examine ourselves to see how we measure up. If we will do that, we will not be condemned by God. If we examine ourselves and determine that we are the cause of the problem, then we are obligated to change our behavior and restore balance and order where it has been disrupted. If the fault is not ours, however, but that of a continual troublemaker, then it may well mean that the person responsible must be removed in order to assure peace and tranquility. When strife is removed from an environment, then everything will begin to flow smoothly again. Harmony will be restored.

But is there anything positive that can be done to insure peace and harmony in our lives? Proverbs 18:24 says, "A man that hath friends must show himself friendly: and there is a friend that sticketh closer than a brother." If you are a born-again Christian and are having trouble in your relationships with other people, then perhaps you need to heed this wise counsel from Solomon. If you don't have friends, start working at it. Take the initiative. Improve your personality. Be friendly. Show more kindness, demonstrate more respect for the opinions of others. Be less critical and demanding. Talk less and listen more. Become interested in someone besides yourself. Put the other fellow first for a change.

Of course, all this will take effort. That's the whole point. One reason sluggards don't have friends is because they're too lazy to work at it. Lazy people want *you* to be their friend, but they don't want to return the favor. They expect you to do all the giving, all the work of building a relationship. To *have* friends, you must *be* a friend.

But even if your efforts at friendship are rejected, you shouldn't despair or give up. There is one who will never reject your offer of friendship. He will always reciprocate and help build a good close relationship. His name is Jesus, and He sticks even closer than a brother. Even if the whole world turns against you, Jesus will still be there by your side to strengthen, comfort and believe in you. He will never leave you nor forsake you.

5

My Son
Proverbs 6:20-23; 3:1-26

With this chapter we begin a series of several lessons on the proper instruction of children. We will be considering how to bring them up in the nurture and admonition of the Lord. Each of the remaining lessons in this series will attempt to reveal the personality and character traits of a certain type individual which it would do well for our children to learn to beware of. Chapter 6 will deal with evil men. Chapter 7 treats the subject of evil women. Chapter 8 discusses what the Bible refers to as the "foolish woman."

In this first chapter on the subject of children, we will consider some of the basic principles involved in Christian child-rearing, using as our example the instructions which our Heavenly Father gives to us as His children. In the Bible the Lord has made it clear that we are not only to heed and obey His commandments to us, we are also to teach these commandments to our "seed." The Lord has told us to fill them with the Word so that when they go out into the world, out from under our influence and control, they will be kept by that Word.

As Christian parents, we need to be obedient to this command. We need to study the Word of God with our children in family devotions and in prayer and sharing times. We must be diligent to see that the Word of God is ingrained in them, for it is their guarantee of a happy and successful life.

Builder of the Family Name—
PROVERBS 6:20-23

My son, keep thy father's commandments, and forsake not the law of thy mother:

Bind them continually upon thine heart, and tie them about thy neck.

When thou goest, it shall lead thee; when thou sleepest, it shall keep thee; and when thou awakest, it shall talk with thee.

For the commandment is a lamp; and the law is light; and reproofs of instruction are the way of life.

"My son..." (v. 20a). Notice to whom this passage of scripture is addressed. That phrase "my son" is found sixteen times in the book of Proverbs. That is because Proverbs is instruction to children.

"...keep thy father's commandments, and forsake not the law of thy mother" (v. 20b). Solomon learned his wisdom at the feet of David and Bathsheba. That's why there are so many admonitions in this book to listen to the teachings of your mother and the instructions of your father. Solomon knew the value of parental guidance and counsel. He had sat at the feet of his own parents and learned directly from them the Word of God. And he had found that the Word was true.

Now to the ancient Hebrew, the term "son" meant "the builder of the family name." That's why sons were so carefully instructed in the ways and values of their father. Because they were seen as the future standard bearers of the family name and all it stood for. In Proverbs 22:1 Solomon wrote: "A good name is rather to be chosen than great riches..." It is important that we teach our children that they are carrying on the family name. They need to be made aware of their responsibility to preserve and protect that "good name."

If you have a son, it is your duty to instruct him in the family code, to make sure he realizes what your family name stands for—the Word and precepts of God. Let him know that he is carrying on an example of that Word.

You see, building a name never stops. We must take what our parents built into us and build upon it, passing it on to our children. They in turn will build upon what we have put in them and will pass that heritage on to their children. And on and on. The building never ceases.

Wisdom is always built on wisdom. Knowledge upon knowledge. Line upon line, and precept upon precept. (Is. 28:10.) As we continue to teach our children, laying a foundation of truth and honor and integrity in them, they will go out into the world and maintain those precepts in their lives. They will lead fuller, happier, healthier, more abundant and fruitful lives than we have lived. They will have more wisdom and knowledge to draw upon and build upon than we did. Then they will continue that building by passing on the foundation they received from us, plus that which they have built upon that foundation in their lifetime. So their children will have an even greater structure and formation from which to benefit and upon which to add their own contribution.

The children of God are always in a "building program." Because the edifice of wisdom is never completed. The building goes on growing forever and ever, each succeeding generation adding to it by passing on "that which it also received." (1 Cor. 15:3.)

The Way of Life—

Let's review Proverbs 1 for a moment. Remember that the word "wisdom" had to do with "pounding in." Wisdom doesn't fall upon us like rain from the sky. It comes as a result of continually applying ourselves to the Word of the Lord. In Proverbs 1:8,9 the Lord says: "My son, hear the instruction of thy father, and forsake not the law of thy mother: for they shall be an ornament of grace unto thy head, and chains about thy neck."

Here the builder of the family name is admonished to heed the instruction of his father. You will recall from our earlier studies that "instruction" means discipline. The word "law" in this passage refers to teaching. So here we find a principle that is repeated throughout the book of Proverbs: The mother teaches the children and the father disciplines. That is logical. The mother is with the children all day long, while the father is on the job. It's important for the children to learn the Word of God from their mother during the day. When "disciplinary" action is called for, it is usually the father who handles it. Now that does not mean that the children should regard their father as the big "ogre" whom the mother calls in to punish them. (And certainly not the one she *threatens* them with!) It just indicates a general "division of labor" in most families based on the basic difference between women and men. Generally mothers tend to "teach" with words, while most fathers "instruct" more by their actions and example than they do by direct indoctrination.

But both teaching and instruction are needed to adequately "train up a child in the way he should go." The key word here is *discipline*. But there is a difference between discipline and punishment. Most people use those words interchangeably. That is a mistake. Punishment is a negative action taken—often *in anger*—to REPAY wrong behavior. Discipline is a positive action taken—*in love*—to PREVENT or CORRECT wrong behavior. The Lord never punishes His children; rather, He "chastens" or disciplines them: "For whom the Lord *loveth* he chasteneth..." (Heb. 12:6). The Lord *punishes* sinners. They are the object of His wrath and vengeance. Only the Lord is allowed to punish: "Vengeance is mine; I will repay, saith the Lord" (Rom. 12:19).

Never correct your child in anger. The rod is for discipline and love, not punishment and vengeance. When used in love, it brings the child back to the right way. Punishment will only build up anger and discouragement. (Col. 3:21.) Discipline reinforces positive values in a child and produces joy and "the peaceable fruit of righteousness" (Heb. 12:11).

"*For thy commandment is a lamp; and the law is light; and reproofs of instruction are the way of life*" (v. 23). The only true way to happiness, health, prosperity, and peace of mind is to lead a disciplined life. The word "discipline" comes from a Latin root meaning "to LEARN." A "disciple," for example, is actually a LEARNER. In Matthew 11:29 Jesus called upon the people of His day to follow Him, saying: "Take my YOKE upon you, and LEARN of me..." His "yoke" referred to His way of life, the way of discipleship. In it's truest sense then, to "discipline" is "to develop by *instruction* and *exercise*; to train in *self*-control or *obedience to given standards* (*Webster's New Collegiate Dictionary*, emphases mine.) And what is the "given standard" to which we are to "train" and "instruct" and "exercise" our children to give "obedience"? The Word of God, of course. The "way of life."

Bound by the Word—

"For they shall be an ornament of grace unto thy head, and chains about thy neck" (Prov. 1:9). Notice that instruction and law (the Word of God) are pictured as an ornament on the head and as chains on the neck. The mind of our children is in their head. So the Word will keep watch over their thoughts. Notice also what kind of thoughts it will produce—thoughts of grace. They will look at the whole world through the grace of God.

The grace of God never looks at "me." It always looks to meet the needs of others. If your child's mind is filled with the Word and grace of God, he will never be a detriment to society, he'll be a tremendous asset. Employers will pass over a hundred people to hire him because they will recognize that he is considerate, that he puts others first, that he is honest, reliable and trustworthy. That he has a clean mind and a pure heart.

There is coming a day when each of us must turn our children loose. We must allow them to go out into this world and make their own way. There is no need to face that moment with fear and apprehension in our heart. If we have raised those children in the Word of God, that Word will be an ornament of grace to their minds. It will keep them better than we ever could.

This verse goes on to say that the Word is like chains about the neck. The "chains" here in the Hebrew are actually chains of gold. That doesn't mean that the Word will be just a decoration like a necklace. We put a chain around a dog's neck to serve as a leash. That leash is for guidance and restraint. What are the chains around the neck of our children for? The same thing. We won't always be there to lead, guide and control them, but the Word will be. It will say to them, "This is the way, walk ye in it" (Is. 30:21).

Children need to have the fullness of the Word on the inside of them. What we teach our children at home and in church is important to them because one day they must go out on their own and face the world alone. But no matter how evil the world becomes, the Word will still be greater. Where sin abounds, grace doth much more abound. (Rom. 5:20.) And it will continue to abound for our children. Whatever comes their way in the future, they are bound to succeed because they are bound to the Word!

Blessings of the Word—

PROVERBS 3:1

My son, forget not my law; but let thine heart keep
my commandments;

Again we find this expression, "my son." This passage is addressed to the "builder of the family name." In it, the Lord is instructing us in what we are to teach our children: not to forget His law but to keep His commandments in their heart. Why? What good does it do to be faithful to the Lord and His Word? Verses 2 through 26 of this chapter contain the blessings that come upon the person who does not forget the Word. Let's look at some of these blessings.

Divine Life—

VERSES 2,3

For length of days, and long life, and peace, shall they add to thee.

"For length of days, and long life..." (v. 2). What is the difference between length of days and long life? They seem to be the same thing, but they're not. Long life refers to life on earth. The patriarchs had long life. Some lived 120, 130 years or more on the earth. This is one of the rewards of keeping the commandments. Do you recall the only one of the Ten Commandments which had a promise attached to it? Paul referred to it in Ephesians 6:2,3: "Honour thy father and mother; which is the first commandment with promise; that it may be well with thee, and thou mayest live long on the earth." Long life is one of the blessings that come from honoring earthly parents as well as our Heavenly Father. Teach that truth to your children.

But what is length of days? Have you ever had days that just didn't seem long enough? You just couldn't quite get everything done that you needed to accomplish. You wished you could expand the day by a few hours to allow you to get caught up. That's what this phrase refers to. Lengthening the day so there is more time available. Do you know why there never seems enough time in your day? It's probably because you have been neglecting the Word. If you will put priority back on the Word, those extra hours will be restored to you. That too is one of the blessings promised to those who forsake not mercy and truth.

Divine Favor—

VERSES 3,4

Let not mercy and truth forsake thee: bind them about thy neck; write them upon the table of thine heart:

So shall thou find favour and good understanding
in the sight of God and man.

"*...bind them about thy neck; write them upon the table of
thine heart*" (v. 3). Notice that there are two things we are
supposed to do with the Word—bind and write. To bind
means to tie. Why are we to tie the Word of God around
our neck? So it won't break loose. In other words, to make
sure the Word is secure in us.

We are also to write it on our heart. This reminds us
of the words of the Lord in Jeremiah 31:33: "But this shall
be the covenant that I will make with the house of Israel;
After those days, saith the Lord, I will put my law in their
inward parts, and write it in their hearts; and will be their
God, and they shall be my people." Twice in the book of
Hebrews this same scripture is referred to. (Heb. 8:10; 10:16.)
What it tells us is that we who are under the new covenant
are supposed to ALREADY have that Word written in our
heart. We just need to learn to listen to the voice of the Spirit
of God within our heart and to be obedient to what He tells
us. If we will, there is promised us another blessing which
is found in verse 4.

"*So shall thou find favour and good understanding in the
SIGHT of God and man*" (v. 4). When we are diligent to learn
and obey the Word of God, we are promised observable favor
with God and man. Notice that God is mentioned first. He
must always be first in our lives if we are to expect to be
first with Him. Jesus taught us to seek FIRST the kingdom
of God, promising that THEN all the things we need would
be added to us. (Matt. 6:33.) And Luke 2:52 tells us that
"Jesus increased in wisdom and stature, and in favor with
God and man." If you increase in favor with God, you *will*
increase in favor with men. Put God first in your life and
He will see to it that you come out on top in the natural
things of life. That is one of the blessings of faithfulness.

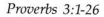

Proverbs 3:1-26

Divine Direction—

VERSES 5,6

Trust in the Lord with all thine heart; and lean not unto thine own understanding.

In all thy ways acknowledge him, and he shall direct thy paths.

"Trust in the Lord with all thine heart..." (v. 5). This passage stresses the importance of turning everything in our lives over to the Lord—even the small details of life. Teach your children that it is the small foxes that spoil the vine. (Song of Sol. 2:15.) Teach them to turn over to the Lord both the great and the small concerns of their daily existence.

"...and he shall direct thy paths" (v. 6). Notice that this is in the future tense. This is a promise from the Lord that He will provide guidance to those who turn their whole lives over to Him in complete trust. Sometimes it may appear that the Lord is falling down on His part of the bargain. Things may not be going all together well for us or our children whom we have committed to the Lord's keeping. It may seem contrary to common sense to keep on believing that all will turn out for the best when we can see with our own eyes that everything is falling totally apart. That's why we are admonished to *trust* in the Lord with all our heart and not to lean to our own understanding. In Jeremiah 29:11 the Lord tells us: "For I know the thoughts that I think toward you, saith the Lord, thoughts of peace, and not of evil, to give you an expected end." That "expected end" is victory! This is also a promise from the Lord to those who put their trust in Him.

Divine Health—

VERSES 7,8

Be not wise in thine own eyes: fear the Lord, and depart from evil.

It shall be health to thy navel, and marrow to thy bones.

"It shall be health to thy navel,..." (v. 7a). The navel, in the center core of the body, speaks of the inward man. This phrase has reference to spiritual life. It is saying that the Word of God will prosper us spiritually.

"...and marrow to thy bones" (v. 7b). The marrow is where the physical blood is produced. It speaks of physical health, the health of the outward man. Not only does the Word of God benefit us spiritually, it also benefits us physically. Psalm 103:2,3 speaks of this dual blessing: "Bless the Lord, O my soul, and forget not all his benefits: who forgiveth all thine iniquities; who healeth all thy diseases." The Word of God prospers inwardly and outwardly. It's health to the whole man—spirit, soul and body. That too is one of the blessings of the Word.

Divine Prosperity—

VERSES 9,10

Honour the Lord with thy substance, and with the firstfruits of all thine increase:

So shall thy barns be filled with plenty, and thy presses shall burst out with new wine.

"Honour the Lord with thy substance,....so shall thy barns be filled with plenty..." (vv. 9,10). This passage tells your children how to be blessed and prosperous throughout their lifetime. Remember that David taught this to his son. Did it work for Solomon? Of course it did. This man was renowned throughout the then-known world for his tremendous wealth. So here we have the counsel of a man who knows from personal experience that what he says is true. This is not theory, it's proven fact! As Solomon testifies here, when you give to the Lord, He always gives back more than was given. Prosperity in abundance is the heritage of those who honor the Lord with their substance.

Divine Correction—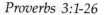

VERSES 11,12

My son, despise not the chastening of the Lord; neither be weary of his correction:

For whom the Lord loveth he correcteth; even as a father the son in whom he delighteth.

"My son, despise not the chastening of the Lord;....for whom the Lord loveth he correcteth..." (vv. 11,12). This passage tells the child that the Lord will sometimes "chasten" him just as a good earthly father spanks his child when necessary. But the child is counseled not to become angry at his Heavenly Father.

Because He loves us, God disciplines us. He corrects us to get us back on course. Earthly fathers spank with the rod. But God "spanks" with the Word. He "scourgeth every son" with "all scripture" which is given "for reproof, for correction, for instruction in righteousness." (Heb. 12:6; 2 Tim. 3:16.)

Job 5:17 says, "Behold, happy is the man whom God correcteth: therefore despise not thou the chastening of the Almighty." Divine correction is another of God's rich blessings which He has provided His children so they "...may be perfect (mature), throughly furnished unto all good works" (2 Tim. 3:17).

Divine Happiness—

VERSES 13-18

Happy is the man that findeth wisdom, and the man that getteth understanding.

For the merchandise of it is better than the merchandise of silver, and the gain thereof than fine gold.

She is more precious than rubies: and all the things thou canst desire are not to be compared unto her.

Length of days is in her right hand; and in her left hand riches and honour.

Her ways are ways of pleasantness, and all her paths are peace.

She is a tree of life to them that lay hold upon her: and happy is everyone that retaineth her.

"Happy is the man that findeth wisdom,.... and happy is everyone that retaineth her" (vv. 13,18). What does it take to make you happy? Would you think that a long and productive life filled with riches, honor, pleasure, and peace might tend to make you happy? Does that sound good to you? Is that what you've been looking for all these years? If so, then I have good news for you. These are precisely the things which are PROMISED to you as a child of God!

More correctly, these are the blessings which are promised to the child of God who "findeth wisdom" and "retaineth her."

Divine happiness is the destiny of all those who earnestly seek God's wisdom and His understanding.

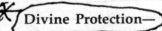 Divine Protection—

VERSES 19-26

The Lord by wisdom hath founded the earth; by understanding hath he established the heavens.

By his knowledge the depths are broken up, and the clouds drop down the dew.

My son, let not them depart from thine eyes: keep sound wisdom and discretion.

So shall they be life unto thy soul, and grace to thy neck.

Then shalt thou walk in thy way safely, and thy foot shall not stumble.

When thou liest down, thou shalt not be afraid: yea, thou shalt lie down, and thy sleep shall be sweet.

Be not afraid of sudden fear, neither of the desolation of the wicked, when it cometh.

For the Lord shall be thy confidence, and shall keep thy foot from being taken.

"Be not afraid of sudden fear, neither of the desolation of the wicked, when it cometh" (v. 25). We need to teach our children to beware. Not to fear, but to be on their guard. There is a difference.

When we say that they will have favor with God and man, that is true. But it is also true that they will NOT have favor with Satan, the god of this world. Because Satan is the enemy of God, he plots against us, God's children. Jesus taught that the devil "cometh not, but for to steal, and to kill, and to destroy" (John 10:10). And he especially tries to rob, kill and destroy Christians. That's why we and our children must be constantly vigilant to make sure that we give him no opportunity to overcome us.

One way Satan comes against believers is by stirring up other people against us. There will always be a certain portion of the world who will oppose us at every turn. And not only will they oppose us, they will despise us and everything we stand for. Because just as God has His children, so does the devil. Jesus said to the Pharisees, "Ye do the deeds of your father....Ye are of your father the devil, and the lusts of your father ye will do. He was a murderer from the beginning, and abode not in the truth, because there is no truth in him..." (John 8:41,44). The children of Satan are still with us today. Our children need to know how to recognize them and how to deal with them.

Proverbs 26:2 says, "As the bird by wandering, as the swallow by flying, so the curse causeless shall not come." This verse is speaking of the children of Satan who try to curse Christians. No one but a fool would do that! Anyone ought to know that you don't tamper with God's property.

The Hebrew word for the first bird mentioned here indicates that it is the sparrow. Sparrows have no permanent home, they wander from one place to another. The distinguishing characteristic of the second bird, the swallow, is that it always returns to the place from which it left. We have all heard of the famous swallows of San Juan Capistrano in California who each year at a certain time return from their migration to settle in one particular old Spanish mission church. The word "come" here actually means "light" or "land."

The reason that only a fool would pronounce a curse upon a Christian is because not only will it not "light" upon the Christian, it will actually return to "land" upon the head of the one who sent it out! Like a sparrow it will wander aimlessly around for a while, then like a swallow it will return to the very place from which it left. Like a boomerang, it will come back upon the curser.

That's why we Christians need have no fear of the world or its plans. Some Christian people are constantly in an uproar over government legislation to outlaw this or ban that. We need to pray for our country and its leaders. We need to let our legislators know how we feel on issues. But we do not need to become "caught up" in fighting our own government.

Those foolish enough to plot against us will live to regret it; all their curses will fall back on their own heads. As Christians it is not our job to fight our fellow man. We are not sent into all the world to fight sin, but to save sinners. The devil is real and he is out there plotting against us, that is true. But the best way to overcome him is by staying in the Word of God and in prayer, and by speaking out at the right time and in the proper way. The Church is built by Jesus Christ and "the gates of hell shall not prevail against it" (Matt. 16:18). When Satan tries to send his curse upon the Church, it won't harm us. It will return upon the one who sent it.

"For the Lord shall be thy confidence, and shall keep thy foot from being taken" (v. 26). Teach your children not to be afraid. Teach them that they don't have to be concerned about what the world thinks or says or does. Despite the world's plotting, no matter how powerful our enemies may become, regardless of what we may see or hear, we will be kept safe. Teach them to walk in confidence because greater is He who is in them than he who is in the world. (1 John 4:4.)

Proverbs 26:27 says, "Whoso diggeth a pit shall fall therein: and he that rolleth a stone, it will return upon him." How wasteful it is for the Church of Jesus Christ to spend all its time fighting this threat or that. Stick to the calling of God and watch Satan fall into his own trap. He will be crushed by the very stone he tried to roll down upon us. The word "pit" here also refers to a grave. Graves are for dead people. Many people think we Christians are easy game. They will end up buried in that same pit they dug for us, just as Haman was hanged on the very gallows he had built for righteous Mordecai. (Esther 7:10.)

Divine protection is one of the blessings of the wise.

Divine Order—

We began this chapter with this verse: "My son, keep thy father's commandment, and forsake not the law of thy mother" (Prov. 6:20). Notice that there is an order here. It is the father who is the commander in the family, the head of the home. The mother is the teacher or lawgiver. Teach your children to respect this order. Teach the boys to be the head of their home, to love their wife, to treat their children right and not to neglect their discipline. Teach the girls to respect their husband and to be the teacher in the home, to be faithful to instruct the children in the way and the Word of the Lord.

That home is blessed which recognizes and respects the divine order instituted by God.

Divine Presence—

"Bind them continually upon thine heart, and tie them about thy neck" (Prov. 6:21). We said that if we do not forsake the Word of God it will not forsake us. It will always be there with us in time of adversity.

"When thou goest, it shall lead thee; when thou sleepest, it shall keep thee; and when thou awakest, it shall talk with thee" (Prov. 6:22). David taught Solomon that he would not always be under his mother and father's roof. There was going to come a day when he would be out on his own. David's counsel to his son was this: Don't forsake the law of your mother or the instructions of your father. That way when you do go out into the world, you will not be alone. The Word will be with you. When you *go*, it will lead you. When you *sleep*, it will watch over you. When you *awake*, it will talk with you.

How many times do parents send their children out into the world afraid of what might happen to them? David knew how to prepare his son for that day. He taught him that wherever he was, whatever he was doing—whether he was asleep or awake—the Word would always be right there with him!

John tells us that Word of God is a Person. (John 1:14.) We need have no fear for our children. Not if they are full of the Word of God. Because whatever they may do, wherever they may go, the Word will be their constant companion. He will never leave them nor forsake them.

Of all the blessings of wisdom, this is the greatest—the Divine Presence of God Himself!

6

Wicked Men

Proverbs 4:10-26; 24:15-18

Hear, O My Son...

PROVERBS 4:10-13

Hear, O my son, and receive my sayings, and the years of thy life shall be many.

I have taught thee in the way of wisdom; I have led thee in right paths.

When thou goest, thy steps shall not be straightened; and when thou runnest, thou shalt not stumble.

Take fast hold of instruction; let her not go: keep her, for she is thy life.

"I have taught thee in the way of wisdom; I have led thee in right paths" (v. 11). As Christians we need to be aware of the devil and his devices. We need to know how to identify and overcome evil. We also need to pass that knowledge on to our children. We dare not send them out into this world thinking that the Lord will teach them what is right and wrong once they're out there. To leave their instruction to God is the lazy way out. It is also dangerous. Children need to be taught about life now, BEFORE they leave home.

"Take fast hold of instruction; let her not go: keep her; for she is thy life" (v. 13). The Bible says that we are to teach our children at home. We are not to leave their instruction to the school or the church. It is *our* responsibility as parents to prepare our children for life. It is *our* duty to instruct them

in the Word of the Lord, the way of life. We are the ones charged with the responsibility of disciplining them, training them up in the way they should go. We do that while they are young; THEN when they get older they will not depart from it. If we will train up our children wisely, the Lord will honor that training and will bear witness of the truth to their spirits by the Word we have implanted in them.

The Path of the Wicked—

VERSES 14-18

Enter not the path of the wicked, and go not in the way of evil men.

Avoid it, pass not by it, turn from it, and pass away. For they sleep not, except they have done mischief; and their sleep is taken away, unless they cause some to fall.

For they eat the bread of wickedness, and drink the wine of violence.

But the path of the just is as the shining light, that shineth more and more unto the perfect day.

"Enter not the path of the wicked, and go not in the way of evil men." (v. 14). There are many Christians who make the mistake of believing the best of everybody. The Bible gives warning after warning about evil people. In this lesson we will study some of the things Proverbs has to say about evil men. We will learn to recognize and identify them. We will learn about them, who they are, how they act, why they do what they do. We will learn how to avoid falling victim to them and their evil ways. Finally, we will learn how to deal wisely with evil men, how to walk in victory despite the evil which surrounds and beckons to us daily.

The Way of the Wicked—

VERSE 19

The way of the wicked is as darkness: they know not that they stumble.

"The way of the wicked is as darkness..." (v. 19). But who are the "wicked"? To answer that question, let's look at Proverbs 6:12: "A naughty person, a wicked man, walketh with a froward mouth." Here the word "naughty" is translated from the Hebrew word *beliyaal* which means "worthless." The naughty person is a child of Satan.

In 2 Corinthians 6:15 the Apostle Paul used the Greek form of this word when he wrote to the church in Corinth: "And what concord hath Christ with Belial?" Strong defines this Greek word as *"worthlessness"* and notes that it was used "as an epithet of Satan."

The name "Satan" does not appear in any of the first twelve books of the Old Testament. Yet the devil is there; he is just called by different names. In Deuteronomy 13:13 for example the Lord warned the children of Israel about being led astray by "the children of Belial." Satan is also referred to by this name in the books of Judges, 1 and 2 Samuel, 1 Kings, and 2 Chronicles. When the children of Israel came into the Promised Land, God warned them that if they did not remove the inhabitants of that land from their presence, then those left would be as pricks in their eyes and thorns in their sides. (Num. 33:55.) This is where Paul got his analogy of the thorn in his flesh, a Satanic messenger sent to "buffet" him. (2 Cor. 12:7.) So in this verse we see that we are not dealing just with unbelievers here, but with those who are Satanic—wicked and evil.

But what is the "way of the wicked"? Again Proverbs instructs us. Verse 13 of Proverbs 6 tells us, "He winketh with his eyes, he speaketh with his feet, he teacheth with his fingers." The wicked man tries to entice people. He uses everything at his disposal to lure and draw them into sin. He speaks with his feet—that is, his feet are always moving. He can't stand still. He speaks with his fingers. Evil signs are nothing new, they were around in Solomon's time. The wicked man uses his body to express his evil intentions.

Evil women are the same way. The same devil controls both. Proverbs 7:11 says of the evil woman: "She is loud and stubborn; her feet abide not in her house." The evil woman cannot stay home, she is always restless. In Matthew 12:43 Jesus tells us that demons are always roaming through the desert or dry places. The devil's people are unstable, always shuffling and moving about, always restless.

Verse 12 said that the wicked man walks with a "froward" mouth. In the Hebrew, this means a perverted mouth. This does not mean to imply that everyone who curses occasionally or uses the Lord's name in vain is necessarily wicked or demon-possessed. But a vile mouth is one of the evidences of wickedness. Jesus taught us that "out of the abundance of the heart the mouth speaketh" (Matt. 12:34). One good indication of what is on the inside of a person is what is manifested on the outside, what comes forth from his mouth.

We meet this kind of people all the time. They constantly use gross and foul language. They find some favorite vulgar phrase and throw it into every sentence. They can't put three words together without having to resort to an obscenity. They do that because that's the way they think. Their mind supplies their mouth with the words that are stored up in their heart. And a heart full of filth and vulgarity is not filled with the Spirit of God.

So teach your children to be observant of other people's behavior and speech. They will soon learn to detect those who are not full of the Word of the Lord, those who are not in tune with the mind and heart of God.

We are often warned not to go by our senses, but to go by faith. But the more we go by faith, the more our senses are exercised to discern between good and evil. (Heb. 5:14.) The more you and your children operate by faith and the Word, the more your eyes will be made able to distinguish between right and wrong, good and evil. The filter for your eyes is the Word of God. The filter for your ears is the Word. Stay in the Word, and you will soon begin to be able to detect people's motives by just observing them. That's what the Lord is saying to us in this passage: "Son, just watch. This is how a sinner gives himself away. First, he walks with a perverted mouth. Then he acts out in his body the restlessness and instability of his spirit. When you see that kind of evidence, beware of that person; his is the way of the wicked."

The End of the Wicked—

"Frowardness is in his heart, he deviseth mischief continually; he soweth discord.

"Therefore shall his calamity come suddenly; suddenly shall he be broken without remedy" (Prov. 6:14,15).

"...*he deviseth mischief continually...*" (v. 14). Notice this word "continually." It means day and night. Do you remember how often we are to meditate in the Word according to Joshua 1:8? "This book of the law shall not depart out of thy mouth; but thou shalt meditate therein *day and night*, that thou mayest observe to do according to all that is written therein..." How often is Satan at work inside the wicked, plotting and devising schemes against God's elect? Continually.

You see, that's why we need to be vigilant, to be constantly alert and on guard. Why we need to be continually in the Word. Because our enemy is open for business 24 hours a day, seven days a week! Satan has at least one virtue—he's not lazy! He's on the job 365 days a year. Day and night the devil is busy scheming and plotting evil against us. That's why God warns us to stay in that Word day and night. He knows that we can't afford to let down our guard for a minute.

"*Therefore shall his calamity come suddenly...*" (v. 15). But notice that the wicked man eventually finds his downfall.

Even though we have seen the wicked prosper, and perhaps have even become envious of them, we should never be tempted to join them in their evil ways. Because sooner or later that way inevitably leads to destruction. Never be envious or jealous of the wicked. Although it may seem that God leaves them alone to grow rich and fat by exploiting the poor and needy, He has not forsaken the downtrodden nor will the wicked flourish indefinitely—their day is coming.

In Psalm 92:7 David tells us, "When the wicked spring as the grass, when all the workers of iniquity do flourish; it is that they shall be destroyed for ever." And Peter would remind us: "The Lord is not slack concerning his promise, as some men count slackness; but is longsuffering to us-ward, not willing that any should perish, but that all should come to repentance" (2 Pet. 3:9). Which is to say that one reason God allows the wicked to prosper for as long as He does is because He loves them and is not willing that they perish; He is withholding judgment as long as possible in hopes that they may yet come to repentance. The existence of evil men in the world and the fact that they seem to prosper is not evidence of God's unfaithfulness to His children, but of His great love for His enemies! God loves the sinner!

But there are those evil ones who are so possessed of the devil that they try to come against God's Church, His elect. The moment they do that, God's anger is kindled against them because they are tampering with His property. These are the ones who will meet calamity suddenly. They will suddenly be cut off, and that without remedy. That's why we in the Church do not have to fight sin or sinners; God will fight His own battles—and He is much better at it than we are!

The Fall of the Wicked—

PROVERBS 24:15-18

Lay not wait, O wicked man, against the dwelling
of the righteous: spoil not his resting place:

For a just man falleth seven times, and riseth up
again: but the wicked shall fall into mischief.

Rejoice not when thine enemy falleth, and let not
thine heart be glad when he stumbleth:

Lest the Lord see it, and it displease him, and he
turn away his wrath from him.

"Lay not wait, O wicked man..." (v. 15). The wicked man's
days are numbered. It doesn't matter if it looks like the
wicked are prospering. It makes no difference if they have
been connected with crime all their lives and their last days
on this earth are filled with riches and honor. Their day is
still coming. The Righteous Judge will still have the last word.

There is coming a payoff day. In that day you and I will
be so glad that *we* followed the path of righteousness to the
very end and were not diverted towards the way of the
wicked. Righteousness always pays off because God backs
it. Satan backs wickedness, but the wages of righteousness
are always better than the wages of sin.

*"For a just man falleth seven times, and riseth up again: but
the wicked shall fall into mischief"* (v. 16). Once the wicked man
falls, he will never get up. The righteous man may fall seven
times, but he will always rise up again. Teach this to your
children. People say in faith that they're never going to fall.
That's not what the Word of God says. No matter who you
are, if you are human, you *will* fall. We all do. But when
we fall, we get back up again.

But the thing about the wicked is that they fall and never
get up. Once Satan has ground everything out of them that
he can, when they are no longer useful to him, then he casts
them aside and moves on to find another unwitting tool for
his use. Satan has no interest in a used-up sinner. But God
does: "He raiseth up the poor out of the dust, and lifteth
the needy out of the dunghill; that he may set him with
princes, even with the princes of his people" (Ps. 113:7,8).
How great is the love and grace of our God!

Once Satan has drained everything he needs out of a person, he throws them on the garbage heap and walks away. That person is hopeless. On his own, he will never rise again. But that is not true of the Christian: "Though he fall, he shall not be utterly cast down: for the Lord upholdeth him with his hand" (Ps. 37:24). You may have fallen many times. If so, don't become discouraged. God continues to hold you with the right hand of His righteousness. He is always there to forgive and restore. So when you fall, don't wallow in your sin and self-pity. Get back up.

"Rejoice not when thine enemy falleth, and let not thine heart be glad when he stumbleth" (v. 17). This is an admonition to believers. When the wicked finally do fall, we are not to gloat over their downfall. Instead we are to be like our Heavenly Father and show mercy and compassion, just as He does to us when we fall.

"Lest the Lord see it, and it displease him, and he turn away his wrath from him" (v. 18). Here we see what will happen if we take joy in the fall of the wicked—God will direct His anger away from him toward us. Don't seek the downfall of any man. Keep on following God, thanking Him that He always protects your steps. When the wicked have fallen into their own trap, when they have been crushed by the very stone they had meant to roll down upon you, forgive them. Lift them up. Pray for them. Witness to them. In so doing, you will be like your Father in heaven who makes His rain to fall upon the just and the unjust and who lifts up all the fallen who call upon Him in faith.

Dealing with the Wicked—

Solomon provides us some practical instruction on how to deal with the wicked people we encounter. In Proverbs 9:7 he writes: "He that reproveth a scorner getteth himself shame: and he that rebuketh a wicked man getteth himself a blot." What does he mean? There are certain types of people we are never to rebuke. One of these types is the totally wicked. These people are so involved in gross sin that they actually flaunt it before the world. They openly slander Christianity and hold Christians up to scorn and ridicule.

When you meet such a person as this, never try to rebuke him. Don't return evil for evil, cursing for cursing. You will be held accountable on the day of judgment for what you say to such people. (Matt. 12:36.) "Judge not, that ye be not judged" (Matt. 7:1).

Well, if we are not to judge or rebuke the wicked, what are we to do? Love them. In the same discourse in which Jesus told us not to judge others, He commanded us: "But I say unto you, Love your enemies, bless them that curse you, do good to them that hate you, and pray for them which despitefully use you, and persecute you" (Matt. 5:44). When you come up against a wicked person, love him. Why? Because you are commanded to do so. But more than that. There is a reason behind that command. The truth is that wicked people don't know how to handle love. They are so accustomed to returning evil for evil and cursing for cursing, they don't know what to think when someone doesn't do that to them. Love the person who hates you and he becomes defenseless. After all, it's not that person who hates you. He's just controlled by Satan. He's only doing what comes naturally to him. Don't rebuke someone for doing what is his nature to do. That's like rebuking a dog for barking, a bird for flying, or a fish for swimming. Anger and hatred are just the normal way of life to Satan's children.

Rather than reacting negatively, instead of doing the very same thing he is doing, show him there is an alternative, a better way. We can't really expect anyone to change his wicked ways until we have first shown him *how* to change. Once his heart is changed through the New Birth, then he will have the desire and the strength to quit doing all those wicked things. Until then we are just wasting our time and breath. Trying to redeem an evil man by rebuking and condemning him is like trying to catch a bird by throwing rocks at it. It just won't work. Instead of changing him, we just make him worse. We must *love* him into the kingdom. Once he's in, then we can begin to teach him the way of the Lord.

As Christians, it is not our job to fight sin in the world or to rebuke the world's sinners. We're not sent to fight but to save. As the old saying goes, "We're not fighters, we're lovers." In 2 Corinthians 5:19 Paul tells us "that God was in Christ, reconciling the world unto himself, not imputing their trespasses unto them; and hath committed unto us the word of reconciliation." In the *New International Version* this verse reads: "...God was reconciling the world to himself through Christ, not counting men's sins against them. And he has committed to us the message of reconciliation." That's the message we have for the world—reconciliation, not condemnation!

The next time you come across a sinner, don't rebuke him—love him. Hate the sin that's in him, but love the sinner. Fulfill your ministry of reconciliation: tell him the good news that God's not counting his sins against him! Then whether he accepts that message or not, even if he goes right on cursing you, leave him with a blessing. Then when you get home, get down on your knees and pray for him. Ask the Lord to reveal Himself through the seeds you have planted. Ask God to grant you more wisdom so that the next time you meet that man you will have more of Jesus to share with him.

Remember: God doesn't kill His enemies, He makes friends out of them! That's the message of reconciliation.

Renew Your Mind—

"My son, keep my words, and lay up my commandments with thee.

"Keep my commandments, and live; and my law as the apple of thine eye.

"Bind them upon thy fingers, write them upon the table of thine heart" (Prov. 7:1-3).

"Keep my commandments...as the apple of thine eye" (v. 2). This expression translated "apple of thine eye" actually refers

to what we would call today the pupil of the eye. What God is saying to each of us here in this passage is this: "Son, look at life through the Word. Let the very pupil of your eye be the Word of God. Whatever you see, examine it through the lens of the Word. See it in My perspective, from My point of view. If people are mistreating you, love them. Pray for them. If things aren't right, the Word will show you what to do. It will tell you when people are right and when they are wrong. It will reveal to you what is in their heart, whether their intentions are honorable or not. Let the Word be the apple of your eye."

"*Bind them upon thy fingers, write them upon the table of thine heart*" (v. 3). Every part of your body should be in obedience to the Word of God, even your fingers. Here God is saying, "Son, people may try to entice you with their eyes, feet, and fingers, but bind the members of your body to My Word. Let every part of you be in obedience to it. Then you will fulfill Romans 12:1, you will be presenting your body as a living sacrifice, holy, and acceptable unto Me."

How do we do that? How do we present our body a living sacrifice to God? By the renewing of our mind through His Word and meditating in it day and night. The more the Word gets into you and renews your mind, the more every part of your body will become obedient to the Word. Jesus will become the Lord of your body. He is already the Lord of your spirit, and more and more you're making Him the Lord of your mind by meditating in His Word. As you do, He will become the Lord of your body also. You will be "sanctifed wholly." (1 Thess. 5:23.)

Ponder Your Path—

PROVERBS 4:20-26

My son, attend to my words; incline thine ear unto my sayings.

Let them not depart from thine eyes; keep them in the midst of thine heart.

For they are life unto those that find them, and health to all their flesh.

Keep thy heart with all diligence; for out of it are the issues of life.

Put away from thee a froward mouth, and perverse lips put far from thee.

Let thine eyes look right on, and let thine eyelids look straight before thee.

Ponder the path of thy feet, and let all thy ways be established.

"For they are life unto those that find them,..." (v. 22a). What is your life?

"...and health to all their flesh" (v. 22b). What is your health?

To the wicked, life is scheming and conniving. What is it to you? To the wicked, security is in riches. Where is your security? To the wicked, wisdom is in themselves, in their own intellect and reason. Where is your wisdom?

The answer to all of these questions is the same: the Word of God. The Word IS your life!

In verses 24 through 26 of this passage the Lord speaks of the mouth and lips, the eyes and eyelids, and the feet. This covers everything we spoke of when we considered the wicked man. His mouth is froward, but we put away a froward mouth. His lips sow discord, but we put away perverse lips far from us. His eyes wink at evil, but our eyes do not depart from the words of God. His feet walk the path of darkness, but our feet follow the path of peace and light. The wicked man makes evil signs with his fingers, but our fingers are bound about with the Word of the Lord. Our hands send God's power into the sick and needy.

And inside it's the same story. The heart of the wicked man is filled with frowardness, but we have written the commandments of our God upon our heart. That's why all our ways are established. Because we guard every part of our being with the Word. That Word keeps us from the way of the wicked which leads to violence and destruction.

One of the most obvious trademarks of a Christian is his peace. The world is restless, sinners must be moving about all the time. But a Christian has peace within. He cannot be shaken. He knows his steps are ordered by the Lord.

If the Lord should come while you are reading these words, if you are a Christian you know that the very next step you take will be upon streets of gold. But even if the Lord tarries, we know that whatever our next step is here on this earth, it is ordained by the Lord. Our physical eye may not see that step, but in our spirit we know that it is there because it is the Lord who directs our path.

Ponder the path of your feet. Enter not into the path of the wicked, but walk in the way of wisdom. If you will do that, you will not stumble in darkness as the wicked, but your way will be established by the Lord and great will be your peace.

7

Wicked Women

Proverbs 6:20-35; 5:1-23; 2:10,11,16-19

Five chapters in Proverbs, Chapters 5 through 9, are a continuation of a thought, a teaching on women and marital fidelity. In Chapter 5 Solomon warns against the "strange woman" (introduced in Chapter 2), exhorting the reader to remain faithful to "the wife of thy youth." The subject of Chapter 6 is the "evil woman," the adulteress. Chapter 7 deals more fully with the "strange woman," the stranger or prostitute. In that chapter, beginning with verse 6, we find the personification of Wisdom as a righteous woman who relates a scene she witnesses from her window as a young man on the street is tempted by a strange woman. In Chapter 8 Wisdom describes herself and the blessedness of those who follow her way, concluding her remarks in Chapter 9 with a comparison between herself and Folly, the foolish woman who represents wickedness.

So there are three types of ungodly women mentioned in Proverbs: 1) The "strange woman," 2) the "evil woman," and 3) the "foolish woman." In this lesson we will discuss the first two of these. In our next lesson we will compare Folly with Wisdom. Then to complete our study of women, in lesson nine we will consider the virtuous woman of Proverbs 31:10-31.

Beware Wicked Women—

PROVERBS 6:20-26

My son, keep thy father's commandment, and forsake not the law of thy mother:

Bind them continually upon thy heart, and tie them about thy neck.

When thou goest, it shall lead thee; when thou sleepest, it shall keep thee; and when thou awakest, it shall talk with thee.

For the commandment is a lamp; and the law is light and reproofs of instruction are the way of life:

To keep thee from the evil woman, from the flattery of the tongue of a strange woman.

Lust not after her beauty in thine heart; neither let her take thee with her eyelids.

For by means of a whorish woman a man is brought to a piece of bread: and the adulteress will hunt for the precious life.

"To keep thee from the EVIL WOMAN, from the flattery of the tongue of a STRANGE WOMAN" (v. 24). Here we see a warning against the two primary types of wicked women. The "evil woman" is the adulteress. The "strange woman" is the prostitute.

"For by means of a whorish woman a man is brought to a piece of bread: and the adulteress will hunt for the precious life" (v. 26). There's a difference between these two types. The "whorish woman," the prostitute, *sells* her body for money. She does what she does to make a living. But the adulteress *gives* herself to her lover. What she does is prompted by a different motive: either to satisfy her own lust, or to exploit the one who falls prey to her charms. The prostitute degrades a man; the adulteress will destroy him. A wise son will avoid both the prostitute and the adulteress.

"Lust not after her beauty in thine heart; neither let her take thee with her eyelids" (v. 25). When the writer of Proverbs warned against consorting with wicked women, he knew what he was talking about. As we have noted, with seven hundred wives and three hundred concubines, no one was

better qualified to speak on the subject of women than Solomon! Besides his own relations with the hundreds of women he came in contact with in his lifetime, Solomon also had the benefit of the counsel of his father David, whose own downfall was caused by his infatuation with the woman Bathsheba, Solomon's mother. We would do well to heed the words of this wise and experienced man.

Our young men must be taught that not all women are like those saints they meet in church, in their youth group or at the prayer breakfast. There are wicked women in this world, women who are backed and controlled by the devil. Just as evil men speak with their body, so these women also have shuffling feet, winking eyes, and seductive fingers. In fact, a wicked woman is much better at communicating with body language than a wicked man!

As we noticed in verse 24, a wicked woman will use "the flattery of the tongue" to entice her victim. Flattery is nothing but perverted praise. Praise desires to put something into a person, to edify *him*. Flattery, on the other hand, seeks to get something out of the person, to edify *self*.

Verses 25 and 26 warn us not to be fooled by the seductive beauty and fluttering eyelids of the wicked woman, for behind them lies a conniving mind and a cruel heart. The wicked woman is out to get something from the man she entices.

Keep Yourself from the Evil Woman—

VERSES 27-35

Can a man take fire in his bosom, and his clothes not be burned?

Can one go upon hot coals, and his feet not be burned?

So he that goeth in to his neighbour's wife; whosoever toucheth her shall not be innocent.

Men do not despise a thief, if he steals to satisfy his soul when he is hungry;

But if he be found, he shall restore sevenfold; he shall give all the substance of his house.

But whoso committeth adultery with a woman lacketh understanding: he that doeth it destroyeth his own soul.

A wound and dishonour shall he get; and his reproach shall not be wiped away.

For jealousy is the rage of a man: therefore he will not spare in the day of vengeance.

He will not regard any ransom; neither will he rest content, though thou givest many gifts.

"Can a man take fire in his bosom, and his clothes not be burned?" (v. 27). When passion arises on the inside of a man, he must put it out before it spreads to the outside. Just as he cannot hold hot coals against his body without being burned, neither can he embrace the wife of another man and walk away unscathed.

"Men do not despise a thief,....but if he be found,...he shall give all the substance of his house" (vv. 30,31). Adultery, the taking of another man's wife, is not like any other theft. If a man steals a loaf of bread and is caught, he can make restitution. Bread is a tangible. It can be paid for. The thief can give something of value to pay off his debt. Once that sum is paid, the debt can be cancelled and forgotten. It's as though the theft never occurred. But when a man commits adultery with another man's wife, there is no price he can pay that will restore that broken marriage relationship. Marital fidelity has no price tag. Like virginity, once lost it can never be restored by paying a fine.

"But whoso committeth adultery with a woman lacketh understanding: he that doeth it destroyeth his own soul" (v. 32).

The man who commits adultery not only destroys a holy union, he destroys his own soul. Now what is his "soul"? It's his mind. Despite what we are told today, there is no such thing as a "victimless" crime. Someone always suffers. Neither is there such a thing as "victimless sin." That's why we are warned about it so strongly. Sin may be covered over, but the deeper it is buried the deeper its roots grow down into the subconscious. A lifetime of guilt and condemnation is a terrible price to pay for a few minutes of adulterous "bliss."

"A wound and dishonour shall he get; and his reproach shall not be wiped away" (v. 33). When a man commits adultery, he sins against his neighbor, his neighbor's wife, and himself—against his own body. (1 Cor. 6:15-20.) And his body will remind him of it for the rest of his life. Besides that, he will lose his reputation. His reproach will always be with him, he'll never be able to wipe the record clean.

"For jealousy is the rage of a man: therefore he will not spare in the day of vengeance. He will not regard any ransom; neither will he rest content, though thou givest many gifts" (vv. 34,35). What will happen when the husband finds out about the adultery? He will be furious. He'll seek vengeance upon the one who defiled his marriage. A broken lamp or vase can be replaced, it can be paid for. What is the price of a broken marriage vow? How much will a man pay a husband for the "use" of his wife? There is no such price. Adultery can never be paid off. The offender can empty his whole house and bank account and still never repay that husband for what he has taken from him. There is no such thing as a "cheap affair"; adultery is one of the most costly things on this earth!

Beware the adulteress. Keep yourself from the evil woman.

Remember Your Covenant—

But there is another reason why the Christian husband should keep himself from adultery. We find it referred to in Job 31:1: "I made a covenant with mine eyes; why then should I think upon a maid?" The word "maid" here means a *virgin*. Not only did Job restrain himself from being led astray by an adulterous woman (an unfaithful married woman), he also covenanted to keep himself from unmarried young ladies. Who did Job make his covenant with? He said he made it with his eyes, but another way of phrasing this sentence is this: "I have taken an oath before God ABOUT my eyes; I have vowed not to even look at another woman." Have you ever done that? Did you not at one time or another stand before a minister of the Lord and solemnly vow to "love and cherish" a certain young woman, pledging to "keep thyself unto her and her only, as long as you both shall live" (or words to that effect)?

Marriage vows are not to be taken lightly. Covenants are not made to be broken or tampered with. Entering into a relationship with another woman—married or single—is not only breaking your sacred oath, it is committing adultery. And that is serious business. The commandment doesn't say, "Thou shalt not have an affair with an adulteress," it says, "Thou shalt not COMMIT adultery" (Ex. 20:14). That's reason enough to keep yourself from the evil woman, even if there never were any harmful effects involved. Because entering into a sexual relationship with any woman other than your wife makes *you* an adulterer. And Hebrews 13:4 tells us, "...but whoremongers and ADULTERERS God will judge"!

In Job 31:9,10, Job made this statement: "If mine heart have been deceived by a woman, or if I have laid wait at my neighbour's door, then let my wife grind unto another, and let others bow down upon her." Job was saying, "If I have taken another man's wife, then let someone else take mine from me." If you are attracted to a woman other than your wife, ask yourself these questions: Would you be willing to grant your wife the same privilege you are contemplating? How would you feel if she were the one being unfaithful? Would it bother you at all to know that your wife was involved in an adulterous affair with another man? Especially if everyone in town knew about it? How would you feel about that man? These are the things you need to consider before you start thinking about how exciting it would be to have a "harmless little affair" with another woman. Especially another man's wife.

"For this is an heinous crime; yea, it is an iniquity to be punished by the judges.

"For it is a fire that consumeth to destruction, and would root out mine increase" (Job 31:11,12).

"For it is a fire that would...root out mine increase" (v. 12). Adultery is designed by Satan to steal your prosperity. It is one of his diabolical schemes to steal from Christians the riches they are receiving as children of God, riches that should be going into the spread of the gospel of Christ. This fact is borne out in Proverbs 29:3: "Whoso loveth wisdom rejoiceth his father: but he that keepeth company with harlots spendeth his substance." A Christian cannot engage in adultery and still continue to prosper.

If that is true, then it's no wonder Satan wants to get us involved in adultery. So he can cause us to lose our prosperity. Then the gospel cannot be carried around the world and preached to every creature. So adultery is costly. Not only to us, but to the kingdom of God. It would do us well to remember that, and to teach our sons to keep themselves from the evil woman.

Avoid the Lips of a Strange Woman—

PROVERBS 5:1-14

My son, attend unto my wisdom, and bow thine ear to my understanding:

That thou mayest regard discretion, and that thy lips may keep knowledge.

For the lips of a strange woman drop as an honeycomb, and her mouth is smoother than oil:

But her end is bitter as wormwood, sharp as a two-edged sword.

Her feet go down to death; her steps take hold on hell.

Lest thou shouldest ponder the path of life, her ways are moveable, that thou canst not know them.

Hear me now therefore, O ye children, and depart not from the words of my mouth.

Remove thy way far from her, and come not nigh the door of her house:

Lest thou give thine honour unto others, and thy years unto the cruel:

Lest strangers be filled with thy wealth; and thy labours be in the house of a stranger;

And thou mourn at the last, when thy flesh and thy body are consumed.

And say, How have I hated instruction, and my heart despised reproof;

And have not obeyed the voice of my teacher, nor inclined mine ear to them that instructed me!

I was almost in all evil in the midst of the congregation and assembly.

"My son, attend unto my wisdom..." (v. 1). Again we find that phrase, "My son." This whole sequence is addressed to the "builder of the family name." Remember, this wisdom is not directed toward the adulteress or the prostitute, but to the child of God. These things may seem to be rather strong to be taught to children, but if introduced to them at the right age, they will understand. The world introduces them to sex early in life through what they see and hear on

television, in movies and at school. Our offspring need to learn about these things at home. They need to be informed about the world we live in, about the temptations they will face in it. They need to know where to draw the line. Teach your children from the Word what is right and wrong. Don't leave it to the school or church to educate your children about these important matters. It's your duty and responsibility to instruct your children in these things. They will benefit from that teaching more when it comes from their parent, and they will also appreciate you for providing it.

"The lips of a strange woman drop as a honeycomb, and her mouth is smoother than oil" (v. 3). Teach your sons, especially, to beware the sweet talk of the evil woman. Warn them against being lead into temptation by the smooth talking seductress. She may look beautiful on the outside, so attractive to the eye and ear, but she is not what she seems. On the inside she is ugly and cheap. She will cheapen and degrade any young man who is foolish enough to fall for her sweet talk and smooth line.

"But her end is bitter as wormwood, sharp as a two-edged sword" (v. 4). Wormwood was a drug used in the ancient world. (Lam. 3:15,19; Amos 5:7.) It produced a terrible hangover and caused brain damage. Consorting with a strange woman will end in destruction of the soul and of the body. Venereal disease and even death are the results of yielding to her charms.

"Her feet go down to death;....her ways are moveable" (vv. 5,6). The evil woman is shifty. Never trust her. Her ways are moveable. The only thing you can depend upon in this life is the unchanging Word of God. Everything else is sand, it will shift on you.

"Remove thy way far from her,....lest thou give thine honour unto others, and thy years unto the cruel: lest strangers be filled with thy wealth;....and thou mourn at the last, when thy flesh and thy body are consumed" (vv. 8-10). Steer clear of the strange

woman. Don't be taken in by her beguiling ways. She will seem so appealing at first, so warm and vibrant and exciting. But her sweetness will turn to bitterness and her warmth to ice. You will end up losing your reputation, your honor, your health and your wealth. Everything you have worked for will be gone, all you own will be forfeited to her. Proverbs 13:22 says, "...the wealth of the sinner is laid up for the just." But Satan comes in to take that wealth away from the just and return it to the sinner. That's why we must not allow ourselves to fall prey to the wiles of the strange woman.

Discretion Shall Preserve Thee—

PROVERBS 2:10,11,16-19

When wisdom entereth into thine heart, and knowledge is pleasant unto thy soul;

Discretion shall preserve thee, understanding shall keep thee:....

To deliver thee from the strange woman, even from the stranger which flattereth with her words;

Which forsaketh the guide of her youth, and forgetteth the covenant of her God.

For her house inclineth unto death, and her paths unto the dead.

None that go unto her return again, neither take they hold of the paths of life.

"Discretion shall preserve thee, understanding shall keep thee" (v. 11). What is it that delivers a person from temptation? Discretion. Understanding. It is the Word of God that delivers from the strange woman and her sweet talk and flattering words.

"Which forsaketh the guide of her youth, and forgetteth the covenant of her God" (v. 17). It is amazing how many of the evil people of this world were raised in church. They have

left their parental guide and have turned their backs on God. That's because they never really received the Word into their heart. They never really met Jesus Christ as their personal Savior, or if they did, they never made a real commitment to Him and His Word. If they had, they wouldn't be involved in such business as seduction and perversity.

The Word will protect you from the strange woman. The Word that is locked in your heart and tied about your neck. The Word that leads you when you walk, watches over you while you sleep, and talks to you when you awake. The Word will guide you far away from the "paths unto the dead" and into the "paths of life."

Rejoice with the Wife of Thy Youth—

PROVERBS 5:15-23

Drink waters out of thine own cistern, and running waters out of thine own well.

Let thy fountains be dispersed abroad, and rivers of waters in the streets.

Let them be only thine own, and not strangers' with thee.

Let thy fountain be blessed: and rejoice with the wife of thy youth.

Let her be as the loving hind and pleasant roe; let her breasts satisfy thee at all times; and be thou ravished always with her love.

And why wilt thou, my son, be ravished with a strange woman, and embrace the bosom of a stranger?

For the ways of man are before the eyes of the Lord, and he pondereth all his goings.

His own iniquities shall take the wicked himself, and he shall be holden with the cords of his sins.

He shall die without instruction; and in the greatness of his folly he shall go astray.

"Drink waters out of thine own cistern, and running waters out of thine own well" (v. 15). This is an obvious exhortation to the believing husband to cling to his wife and to her only. He is not to go seeking "refreshment" from any other source. It is also an admonition to be satisfied with the wholesomeness of the fresh water of marital love and not to seek after the "sweetness" and thrill of "stolen waters." (Prov. 9:17.)

"Let thy fountains be dispersed abroad, and rivers of waters in the streets" (v. 16). The word "fountains" speaks of the righteous man's sexual strength. It is saying to him to be proud, knowing that his children are the products of a right relationship. They are not the offspring of a momentary, adulterous escapade with a strange woman, but are the fruit of the union between a loving husband and wife "whom God hath joined together." As the years go by, they in turn will produce other such fruit, their own children, who will go out like rivers of water to carry the gospel wherever they go.

"Let thy fountain be blessed: and rejoice with the wife of thy youth" (v. 18). Here Solomon urges the believer to hold fast to the one he first married and to find his joy and fulfillment in her. This is not meant to heap condemnation on those who have been divorced and who have since married someone else. What's past is past. The Bible teaches that if we confess our sins, the Lord is faithful and just to forgive us our sins and to cleanse us from ALL unrighteousness. (1 John 1:9.) But, it is true that the Lord Jesus told the woman caught in adultery to go and sin no more. (John 18:11.) Divorce is not the answer to an unhappy marriage. It just compounds the problem.

It takes real discipline to sit down and work out marriage problems. To give up and fall into adultery indicates a lack of self-discipline. It takes courage and determination to stay with a weak marriage and make it work by the help and grace of God. But it is well worth it.

To "rejoice" means to cheer up. That's what a man's wife is for, to cheer him up. Did you know that sex was God's idea and invention? The sexual relationship is one of the most important foundations of a marriage and, like marriage itself, was instituted by God. The way sex is portrayed and flaunted today, you would almost think Satan had designed it. God created sex for the joy of His children. In Genesis we read that in the Garden of Eden the man and his wife were naked and "were not ashamed (embarrassed)." (Gen. 2:25.) In Deuteronomy 24:5 we read these words: "When a man hath taken a new wife, he shall not go out to war, neither shall he be charged with any business: but he shall be free at home one year, and shall cheer up his wife which he hath taken." This expression "cheer up" is the same root word in Hebrew as "rejoice." According to Strong it means to be glad, to be joyful, to make merry. Sex is not just to produce children. God designed it for pleasure as well as for procreation.

"...let her breasts satisfy thee at all times..." (v. 19a). Wife, your breasts are for your husband. They are not something you should be ashamed of or cover or hide from him. In 1 Corinthians 7, Paul tells us that the wife has no more authority over her own body, but the husband does, and vice versa. In the marriage vow, a man and wife give themselves—their body as well as their heart—to each other. There should be no shame or embarrassment between a husband and wife. Paul also teaches that neither should "defraud" the other by withholding sex. (1 Cor. 7:5.)

"...and be thou ravished always with her love" (v. 19b). The word "ravished" in this verse actually means "to be intoxicated or enraptured with." A husband should be enraptured with his wife's love. Her body should thrill him when they make love. God designed it that way, and it is good.

"And why wilt thou, my son, be ravished with a strange woman, and embrace the bosom of a stranger?" (v. 20). Again the admonition to the husband to find his joy, to be enraptured, with his own wife rather than to seek pleasure and fulfillment outside of marriage with a strange woman.

"For the ways of a man are before the eyes of the Lord, ...and he shall be holden with the cords (chains) *of his sins. He shall die without instruction..."* (vv. 21-23). Remember what the word "instruction" means? Discipline. A man will die from lack of self-discipline. If he becomes weighed down in the chains of adultery, it will strangle him. He cannot blame God for his downfall, because it is his own sin that has caused it. He cannot even blame Satan. Although the devil may have laid the trap by providing the temptation, the man gave into that temptation of his own accord. A disciplined person would have resisted temptation and remained safe and free. A man disciplined in the Word will cast down every imagination and bring every thought into captivity to the obedience of Jesus Christ. (2 Cor. 10:5.)

Where do we get our example of how a marriage should operate? From Jesus and the Church. When Jesus entered into a covenant with us, He never broke it. Has God ever gone back on His covenant? Never. Even if we miss it, God will never violate His Word of promise.

In Ephesians 5:22-25 we read:

"Wives, submit yourselves unto your own husbands, as unto the Lord.

"For the husband is the head of the wife, even as Christ is the head of the church: and he is the saviour of the body.

"Therefore as the church is subject unto Christ, so let the wives be to their own husbands in everything.

"Husbands, love your wives, even as Christ also loved the church, and gave *himself* for it."

Husband, what your wife wants most from you is you. You may buy her presents and gifts, but they mean nothing unless you first give *yourself*. What your wife wants is your time, your energy, your companionship. Your *friendship*. I don't have to buy my wife things in order to please her and to keep our love strong. But I do have to be a friend to her.

When we are lonely, we don't really want or need gifts. It's not our mate's *presents* which we yearn for, it's their *presence*! In all your getting, get understanding. And in all your giving, give yourself. That's the greatest gift of all. "For God so loved...that He gave..." And what He gave out of His love was Himself:

"That he might sanctify and cleanse (the church) with the washing of the water by the word.

"That he might present it to himself a glorious church, not having spot, or wrinkle or any such thing; but that it should be holy and without blemish.

"So ought men to love their wives as their own bodies. He that loveth his wife loveth himself" (Eph. 5:26-28).

"*...he that loveth his wife loveth himself*" (v. 28). If that is true, then "he that committeth adultery hateth himself." If you love your wife, you love yourself. If you leave her for another, you are hurting your own body. And you will die from a lack of discipline.

Therefore, don't be led astray by the wicked woman. Rejoice in the wife of your youth!

8
Folly Vs. Wisdom
Proverbs 9:13-18; 7:6-27; 9:1-6

In our last lesson we discussed wicked women: the evil woman (the adulteress) and the strange woman (the prostitute). In this chapter we will consider two other "women": Folly (the foolish woman, representing the seduction of the world) and Wisdom (the virtuous woman, a symbol of the Word of God). We will compare the two to see how they are similar in certain ways, but also how vastly different they are. Finally, we will consider the results of yielding to each of these two "ladies."

The Foolish Woman—

PROVERBS 9:13-18

A foolish woman is clamourous: she is simple, and knoweth nothing.

For she sitteth at the door of her house, on a seat in high places of the city.

To call passengers who go right on their ways:

Whoso is simple, let him turn in hither; and as for him that wanteth understanding, she saith to him,

Stolen waters are sweet, and bread eaten in secret is pleasant.

But he knoweth not that the dead are there; and that her guests are in the depths of hell.

Here, in the person of Folly, the foolish woman who sits in the doorway of her house and lies in wait to seduce the simple, Solomon paints for us a graphic picture of the attractiveness and seductiveness of sin. This woman symbolizes the temptations of the world which tries to lure the simple-minded and gullible into Satan's trap.

"Whoso is simple, let him turn in hither; and as for him that wanteth understanding, she saith to him..." (v. 16). In the Garden of Eden, Satan lured Eve into sin by promising her KNOWLEDGE, the very thing offered here to the simple by the foolish woman. Isn't it strange that the one who is herself stupid, the one who knows nothing, should offer knowledge and wisdom to the simple? The reason Satan and his followers are ignorant is because, as we learned from Solomon, "the fear of the Lord is the beginning of knowledge" (Prov. 1:7). Satan's tactics have not changed; he still tempts the simple into sin and destruction by offering them what he himself does not have.

"Stolen waters are sweet, and bread eaten in secret is pleasant" (v. 17). Like a spider luring a fly into its web, the temptress cries out to the ignorant passersby to come and sample her forbidden wares, implying that it is fun and exciting to be secretive and mysterious.

Here again we are reminded of Satan's original seduction in the Garden: "And when the woman saw that the tree was *good for food*, and that it was *pleasant to the eyes*, and a tree to be desired to *make one wise*, she took of the fruit thereof, and did eat..." (Gen. 3:6). Satan still operates the same today as he did in the beginning; he entices people into his trap by appealing to their desires for sensual pleasure and increased knowledge. He offers them food for their stomachs and "food for thought."

"But he knoweth not that the dead are there; and that her guests are in the depths of hell" (v. 18). The foolish woman promises what she cannot deliver. Her words are false and her motives are evil. And anyone who is foolish enough to succumb to her enticements will end up by being destroyed.

Like Adam and Eve, in the day that he sins by yielding to temptation, he will surely die. Because the ways of the foolish woman are the ways of death and hell.

The Encounter—

PROVERBS 7:6-12

For at the window of my house I looked through my casement.

And beheld among the simple ones. I discerned among the youths, a young man void of understanding.

Passing through the street near her corner; and he went the way to her house.

In the twilight, in the evening, in the black and dark night.

And, behold, there met him a woman with the attire of an harlot, and subtil of heart.

(She is loud and stubborn; her feet abide not in her house:

Now is she without, now in the streets, and lieth in wait at every corner.)

The viewer behind the lattice work is the virtuous woman called Wisdom. She tells what she observed one evening from her window as a young man was met on the street by a prostitute. Note the similarity of this woman and the "strange woman" of our last lesson.

"And, behold, there met him a woman with the attire of an harlot, and subtil of heart" (v. 10). Do you recall the profession of the "strange woman"? She is a prostitute. She earns her living by selling her body. Notice that this woman is dressed "with the attire of an harlot." Notice also that this woman is "subtil of heart." Wisdom can see what the young

man cannot. If he had wisdom in his heart, he too could have discerned the subtle heart behind the flattering tongue.

"She is loud and stubborn; her feet abide not in her house" (v. 11). What did Solomon say about the strange woman in Proverbs 5? "Her feet go down to death; her steps take hold on hell....her ways are moveable, that thou canst not know them" (vv. 5,6). These two verses express the same thought.

"Now is she without, now in the streets, and lieth in wait at every corner)....in the twilight, in the evening, in the black and dark night" (v. 12). What is another name for a prostitute? A streetwalker. And why does she walk the streets "in the twilight, in the evening, in the black and dark night"? To seduce young men into committing adultery with her.

So therefore it seems quite obvious that the seductive woman of Proverbs 7 is the same as the "strange woman" of Proverbs 5. Both of them are symbolic of the very opposite of Wisdom.

But notice also the similarity of this seductive woman of Proverbs 7 and the "foolish woman" of Proverbs 9:13-18. It is clear that they too are the same. Therefore what we have pictured here is not just a story of a young man who falls for the seduction of a prostitute in the street, but a symbolic representation of the age-old battle between sin and righteousness, evil and good, foolishness and wisdom. Between Satan and God.

An Affair to Remember—

Now that we have established who these people are, let's go back and look at this scene from Wisdom's point of view. Although Solomon is recounting this incident by placing his words in the mouth of a woman called Wisdom (Prov. 4:6-8.), we should know by now who the person of Wisdom really is. (Prov. 8:22-31.)

"For at the window of my house I looked...and beheld..." (vv. 6-7a). Notice this: A person might think he is getting away

with something when he sneaks around to engage in an adulterous affair, but there is someone who watches and sees everything he is doing, someone who knows the very thoughts and intents of his heart. That someone also knows the intents of the heart of the seductress, can see her for exactly what she is. That's why these words are written, to teach us how to develop that same capacity so we will choose the path of life rather than the path that leads to death.

"...I discerned among the youths, a young man void of understanding. Passing through the street near her corner; and he went the way to her house" (vv. 7,8). Notice this word "passing." It is probably the most important word in these two verses. In the Hebrew it means "sauntering." That is a key word. This young man wasn't just walking along on his way to some set destination, he was shuffling aimlessly through the streets. What causes young men to wander around the streets at night looking for excitement or adventure? Boredom. I remember when I was in college, how the fellows in the dormitory would go out "cruising" in the evening, drinking beer and driving the streets looking for girls to pick up or "hell raising" to get into. Why? Because they were bored. Boredom is one of Satan's favorite tools. He uses it to create a hunger for excitement which often leads to trouble. Our children need to be taught how to deal with boredom. The solution is found in Proverbs 4:1-8:

"Hear, ye children, the instruction of a father, and attend to know understanding.

"For I give you good doctrine, forsake ye not my law.

"For I was my father's son, tender and only beloved in the sight of my mother.

"He taught me also, and said unto me, Let thine heart retain my words: keep my commandments, and live.

"Get wisdom, get understanding: forget it not; neither decline from the words of my mouth.

"Forsake her not, and she shall preserve thee: love her, and she shall keep thee.

"Wisdom is the principal thing; therefore get wisdom: and with all thy getting get understanding.

"Exalt her, and she shall promote thee: she shall bring thee to honour, when thou dost embrace her."

"Hear, ye children..." (v. 1). Notice that Solomon is not talking to adults here, but to children, to young people.

"Get wisdom, get understanding..." (v. 5) His wise counsel to youth on how to overcome boredom and avoid the snares of Satan is to get wisdom. Can wisdom be obtained overnight? No. How long does it take to "get" wisdom? A week? A month? A year? Or does it take a *lifetime*? God's wisdom is as infinite as He is. That means there will never come a day when we and our children will not need to be studying the Word of God. Getting wisdom and understanding is a lifetime pursuit.

"Forsake her not, and she shall preserve thee: love her, and she shall keep thee....Exalt her, and she shall promote thee: she shall bring thee to honour, when thou dost embrace her" (vv. 6,8). In Proverbs 6:27 Solomon asked this question: "Can a man take fire in his bosom, and his clothes not be burned?" When we studied that verse in our last lesson we said that a man cannot embrace a wicked woman without bringing harm to himself. In this passage Solomon recommends to us a "woman" we can embrace who will bless us rather than harm us. As we hold to her, she holds to us and preserves us. As we love her, she watches over us and protects us. As we exalt her, she promotes us. And when we embrace her, she brings us to honor. Now that's a love affair worth getting involved in! We will meet this lovely lady called Wisdom later on in this lesson. We will also reveal her true identity.

The Seduction—

VERSES 13-21

So she caught him, and kissed him, and with an impudent face said unto him.

I have peace offerings with me; this day have I payed my vows.

Therefore came I forth to meet thee, diligently to seek thy face, and I have found thee.

I have decked my bed with coverings of tapestry, with carved works, with fine linen of Egypt.

I have perfumed my bed with myrrh, aloes, and cinnamon.

Come, let us take our fill of love until the morning; let us solace ourselves with loves.

For the goodman is not at home, he is gone a long journey.

He hath taken a bag of money with him, and will come home at the day appointed.

With her much fair speech she caused him to yield, with the flattering of her lips she forced him.

"*So she caught him, and kissed him,...with an impudent face...*" (v. 13). The word "impudent' here means bold. Notice one thing about this kind of woman: she is brazen. She makes no effort to respect the rules of etiquette and decorum. That should be a clue to us in learning to discern the ungodly woman. Because truly Biblical women are modest, chaste and discreet.

"*I have peace offerings with me; this day have I payed my vows*" (v. 14). The young man appears to have claimed he was a believer. The woman's words here seem to indicate that she was too. "Tonight I have even prayed. God must have brought me just to *you*." If this woman *did* know the Lord, she had forsaken the guide of her youth. That should be a lesson to us. Just because a woman attends church regularly does not necessarily mean that she is a believer, or that she is truly spiritual in her thoughts and actions. Some of the best known sex symbols in Hollywood claim to be "Christian." On the other hand, some "believers" can also be the most devastating tools of Satan.

I have talked to many evangelists who travel from city to city on speaking engagements. Some of them have confided in me that one of the things they have to guard against most is improper advances from women in the churches they visit. They say that there will often be some "lady" from the church who will approach them with this "word from the Lord": "Traveling away from home like you do, I know you must get lonely. God has spoken to me and told me that it is His will that I come to your hotel room with you to take care of your physical needs." I have counseled with people who actually believed that their extramarital affairs were God's will for them. They have told me that the Lord knew how badly they needed love, and since they weren't being satisfied at home, He had sent them a good sex partner to fulfill that need! Such people are deceived by Satan. They bring condemnation upon themselves and shame upon the Church of Jesus Christ.

"With her much fair speech she caused him to yield, with the flattering of her lips she forced him" (v. 21). This young man put up a fight at first, but the woman persisted until she broke his will. He should never have reasoned with her. He should have run. "Flee fornication" is God's command. (1 Cor. 6:18.) Again we are reminded of who this woman is. In Proverbs 6, Solomon warned us to keep our father's commandments and to forsake not the law of our mother because they would keep us "from the evil woman, from the *flattery of the tongue of a strange woman*" (v. 24). And in Proverbs 5:3 he declared: "For *the lips of a strange woman* drop as an honeycomb, and her mouth is smoother than oil." And then he added in the next verse, "But her end is bitter as wormwood..."

The Outcome—

VERSES 22,23

He goeth after her straightway, as an ox goeth to the slaughter, or as a fool to the correction of the stocks;

Till a dart strike through his liver; as a bird hasteth to the snare, and knoweth not that it is for his life.

"He goeth after her straightway,...and knoweth not that it is for his life" (vv. 22-23). A recent newspaper article written by the Associated Press and date-lined Atlanta, Georgia, appeared in the *Tulsa World*. The title of the article was this: **Suicide Rising Problem, Officials Say**. In this article it was noted that "suicide is responsible for one American death every 20 minutes" and that it has become "a serious public health problem in the United States, especially among *young men*." The article went on to declare that suicides were responsible for at least 287,322 deaths in the U.S. between 1970 and 1980: "Nearly three-fourths of those deaths—72.8 percent—occurred among *males*."

"The most striking aspect of the study," the report said was "the dramatic rise in the suicide rate for *young men, in the 15-24 and 25-34 age groups*." The report noted that the suicide rate for that particular group of young men rose 50% in that ten-year period!

About the same time that this article was published, there also appeared in the same newspaper another article noting the alarming increase in the number of cases of genital herpes, especially among teenagers and young adults. The thrust of the report was that this venereal-type disease has reached epidemic proportions, and that it is no longer responding to treatment which has been effective in the past.

It is obvious that something is terribly wrong somewhere when so many of our young men are taking their own life. Unwanted pregnancies, hasty marriages, divorce, abortion, venereal disease—to say nothing of emotional and spiritual breakdowns—all of these "outcomes" of adulterous relationships must have some bearing on the increase in the suicide rate among young people in this nation.

The Warning—

VERSES 24-27

Hearken unto me now therefore, O ye children, and attend to the words of my mouth.

Let not thine heart decline to her ways, go not astray in her paths.

For she hath cast down many wounded: yea, many strong men have been slain by her.

Her house is the way to hell, going down to the chambers of death.

"Hearken unto me now therefore, O ye children, and attend to the words of my mouth" (v. 24). Notice the admonition to *children*.

"Let not thine heart decline to her ways, go not astray in her paths. For....her house is the way to hell..." (vv. 25-26). Was it a mere coincidence that the "Bible Thought" quoted on the masthead of the newspaper the very day the article on suicide appeared was Ecclesiastes 12:13?: *Fear God, and KEEP HIS COMMANDMENTS: for this is the whole duty of man.* I don't think so. The Lord has been trying to warn us to teach our children the dangers of adultery and illicit sex ever since the days of Solomon.

The Wise Woman—

PROVERBS 9:1-6

Wisdom hath builded her house, she hath hewn out her seven pillars:

She hath killed her beasts; she hath mingled her wine; she hath also furnished her table.

She hath sent forth her maidens: she crieth upon the highest places of the city.

Whoso is simple, let him turn in hither: as for him that wanteth understanding, she saith to him.

Come, eat of my bread, and drink of the wine which I have mingled.

Forsake the foolish and live: and go in the way of understanding.

"Wisdom hath builded her house, she hath hewn out her seven pillars" (v. 1). What are the seven pillars of wisdom? Proverbs 6:16-19 tells us that an evil person has seven abominations: A proud look, a lying tongue, hands that shed innocent blood, a heart full of wicked imaginations, feet that are swift in running to mischief, a voice that speaks lies, a mouth that sows discord. These are the seven pillars upon which he has built his house, so that house is going to crumble.

But notice that wisdom also builds a house on seven pillars. What are they? We find them in Proverbs 1:3,4: Wisdom, justice, judgment, equity, subtilty, knowledge and discretion. And the house built on those pillars will never fall. Jesus said that He would build His Church upon a rock, and that the gates of hell would not be able to prevail against it. (Matt. 16:18.) When those pillars become the pillars of your home, of the spiritual home inside you, then nothing in hell can succeed against you.

"She hath killed her beasts; she hath mingled her wine; she hath also furnished her table" (v. 2). You will recall that when the strange woman took someone into her house, there was nothing there except a bed covered with tapestry and scented with perfumes; her house was filled with death. (Prov. 7:16,17,27.) But look at Wisdom's home. She has a table set with elegant tableware and laden with choice meats and fine wines.

"She hath sent forth her maidens: she crieth upon the high places of the city" (v. 3). Notice that Wisdom does not leave her house, but rather remains behind to make final preparations while her servants are sent out to invite the honored guests.

Who is this wonderful person called Wisdom who invites us to come to her banquet table and feast? Wisdom is the Word of God—the Lord Jesus Christ!

Our Lord arose from the dead and went into heaven to prepare a place for us, that where He is there we might be also. (John 14:2,3.) When He ascended on high, He sent forth His "maidens," His servants—He gave some to be apostles, prophets, evangelists, pastors, and teachers—to go out into the highways and byways and to compel people to come in. Why didn't Jesus go Himself? Because He stayed behind to prepare the marriage supper of the Lamb.

My friend, I am a servant in the house of the Lord. He has sent me to tell you to come to the table; all is in readiness. You are invited to the most elaborate and sumptuous banquet that history will ever see. Your place is reserved.

"Whoso is simple, let him turn in hither: as for him that wanteth understanding, she saith to him, Come, eat of my bread..." (vv. 4,5). In the meantime, come on in. Wisdom has a table prepared for you now. And her invitation is almost the same as that of the foolish woman who cries out: "Whoso is simple, let him turn in here; and as for him that wanteth understanding, she saith to him, Stolen waters are sweet, and bread eaten in secret is pleasant" (Prov. 9:16,17). But with one important difference. The bread offered by Wisdom is not stolen. Jesus never had to steal a thing: "The earth is the Lord's, and the fulness thereof; the world, and they that dwell therein" (Ps. 24:1).

There is another difference. Notice what the prostitute offers with her bread. *Water.* But Wisdom offers us *wine.* Through the communion, the bread and wine representing His own body and blood, Christ offers us today eternal life. He offers us health, prosperity, and freedom from the curse which Satan brought upon mankind. Today we walk as free men because the Son has set us free through the work of the cross. And when Jesus sets you free, you are free indeed! (John 8:36.)

Proverbs 9:1-6

Therefore, *"Forsake the foolish and live: and go in the way of understanding."*

9

The Virtuous Woman

Proverbs 31:10-31

PROVERBS 31:10-31

Who can find a virtuous woman? for her price is far above rubies.

The heart of her husband doth safely trust in her, so that he shall have no need of spoil.

She will do him good and not evil all the days of her life.

She seeketh wool, and flax, and worketh willingly with her hands.

She is like the merchants' ships; she bringeth her food from afar.

She riseth also while it is yet night, and giveth meat to her household, and a portion to her maidens.

She considereth a field, and buyeth it: with the fruit of her hands she planteth a vineyard.

She girdeth her loins with strength, and strengtheneth her arms.

She perceiveth that her merchandise is good: her candle goeth not out by night.

She layeth her hands to the spindle, and her hands hold the distaff.

She stretcheth out her hand to the poor; yea, she reacheth forth her hands to the needy.

She is not afraid of the snow for her household: for all her household are clothed with scarlet.

She maketh herself coverings of tapestry; her clothing is silk and purple.

Her husband is known in the gates, when he sitteth among the elders of the land.

She maketh fine linen, and selleth it; and delivereth girdles unto the merchant.

Strength and honour are her clothing; and she shall rejoice in time to come.

She openeth her mouth with wisdom; and in her tongue is the law of kindness.

She looketh well to the ways of her household, and eateth not the bread of idleness.

Her children arise up, and call her blessed; her husband also, and he praiseth her.

Many daughters have done virtuously, but thou excellest them all.

Favour is deceitful, and beauty is vain; but a woman that feareth the Lord, she shall be praised.

Give her of the fruit of her hands; and let her own works praise her in the gates.

It is interesting that the last chapter of Proverbs should deal with the subject of the virtuous woman. Why do you suppose the Lord chose to conclude this book of wisdom by devoting fully half of the final chapter to a discussion of a woman? For 30 and one-half chapters the author of Proverbs has been describing and discussing *wisdom*. Then he culminates his presentation by painting a verbal portrait of the *virtuous* woman. Why? What has virtue to do with wisdom? Obviously the portrayal of this woman must have some relation to the theme of the rest of the book.

The answer is clear: Virtue is the *product* of wisdom. **The virtuous woman is the MANIFESTATION of the wisdom of God.**

Let's examine this important passage carefully then to see what the Lord would have us learn from it. As we do so, keep in mind that the woman called Wisdom represents God's wisdom. Although we will be discussing this passage in terms of the virtues of a Godly wife and her worth to her husband and family, the deeper truth being presented in these verses is *the value of the Word of God to the believer*. What we are really being taught here is what the Word means to us, what it will do FOR US!

The Value of Wisdom—

"*Who can find a virtuous woman? for her price is far above rubies*" (v. 10). What is the price of wisdom? How much would you pay for the Word of God? In Proverbs 3:15 Solomon tells us that wisdom is "more precious than rubies: and all the things thou canst desire are not to be compared unto her." Then in Proverbs 8:11 He repeats this truth, "For wisdom is better than rubies; and all the things that may be desired are not to be compared to it." Here we find this same idea being used to value a virtuous woman. What is this woman worth to her husband? She is priceless, because she is the answer to his prayers, the manifestation of the deepest desires of his heart.

Solomon tells us that "whoso findeth a wife findeth a good thing, and obtaineth favour of the Lord" (Prov. 18:22). This too reminds us of the words of Wisdom in Proverbs 8:34: "For whoso findeth me, findeth life, and shall obtain favour of the Lord."

You probably know that in Old English, from which we get our words "wife" and "woman," there was no distinction between the two, they were the same word (*wif*). But do you know what the word "husband" really means? Of course, it has the commonly accepted meaning of a "male spouse," what Webster calls the "correlative of wife." But it also has another definition, a much older and more basic meaning. The word "husband" is derived from two Old English words "*hus*," meaning house, and "*bonda*" meaning holder. So a "husband" is a householder, the one in charge of a household.

In other words, the husband is more than just the wife's mate; he is the manager of the household. It is the husband who is charged with the responsibility of directing the affairs of the home. So when a man seeks and finds a good wife, it is evidence of two things: 1) Good management on his part, and 2) favor with the Lord, the Proprietor of the Estate. That's why Solomon *recommends* the virtuous woman (Wisdom) as the perfect choice for a wife, and why he *commends* any man who is a wise enough manager to have "found" such a treasure.

But when a Christian "finds" a good wife, it is not actually either just a result of his good management or good luck. In Proverbs 19:14 Solomon says: "House and riches are the inheritance of fathers: and a prudent wife is from the Lord." James tells us that every good and perfect gift comes from our heavenly Father. (James 1:17.) Husbands and wives are gifts to each other from God. We should be more grateful and thankful to God for our mate than we are for our house and wealth.

In Proverbs 8:17 Wisdom cries out: "I love them that love me; and those that seek me early shall find me." Wisdom is available to EVERY believer. Good management consists not so much in "finding" God's gift, but in RECOGNIZING it when we come across it! The virtue is in recognizing the VALUE of God's precious gift of Wisdom, and of availing ourselves of it. Throughout the book of Proverbs that's what Solomon is constantly urging us to do—in all our getting, to get Wisdom! Because nothing we can ever desire can compare to her. She is priceless.

Let me show you what the favor is that you receive from God when you find a good mate. The Bible says in Deuteronomy that if one can put to flight a thousand, then two can chase ten thousand. Did you know that when you get married you instantly increase your faith power ten times? The Lord Jesus told us that if any two shall agree on earth as touching anything they shall ask, it shall be done for them. (Matt. 18:19.) Amos asks, "How can two walk together, except they be agreed?" (Amos 3:3). In the power of agreement between a husband and wife, faith power is multiplied ten times. Any two people can agree and get good results, but I believe the strongest union on earth is marriage, because the Bible says that the two become one flesh.

Some men have told me that they want to go into the ministry but that their wife just doesn't understand. They say, "My wife is so carnal, I'm tempted to just go on into the ministry without her." That is a mistake. If God has called a husband into the ministry, He has also called the wife. Because the two are one. If the wife doesn't feel that call or if she resists it, then the husband needs to begin to pray for her that she will come into agreement with him—on her own. If the call is truly from God, it will happen. It just takes prayer and patience. Plus wisdom.

Wisdom's Provision—

"The heart of her husband doth safely trust in her, so that he shall have no need of spoil" (v. 11). The *New International Version* translates this verse: "Her husband has full confidence in her and lacks nothing of value." That reminds us of David's assurance in Psalm 84:11: "For the Lord God is a sun and shield:...no good thing will he withhold from them that walk uprightly." And Wisdom cries out: "...I...cause those that love me to inherit substance; and I...fill their treasuries" (Prov. 8:21).

"She will do him good and not evil all the days of her life" (v. 12). This recalls God's promise in the *New International*

143

Version of Jeremiah 29:11: "For I know the plans I have for you," declares the Lord, "plans to prosper you and not to harm you, plans to give you hope and a future." And Solomon says of Wisdom: "Length of days is in her right hand; and in her left hand riches and honour" (Prov. 3:16).

Wisdom's Industry—

"*She seeketh..., and worketh willingly....she bringeth....she riseth..., and giveth...*" (vv. 13-15). In this passage we see that the virtuous wife is not like the foolish woman or the sluggard. She works honestly and *willingly* to provide for the needs of her family. Solomon says of Wisdom, "She is a tree of life to them that lay hold upon her: and happy is every one that retaineth her" (Prov. 3:18). And Wisdom herself cries out: "Come, eat of my bread, and drink of the wine which I have mingled."

Wisdom's Business—

"*She considereth a field, and buyeth it: with the fruit of her hands she planteth a vineyard*" (v. 16). This verse tells us that the virtuous wife is also a good businesswoman. Her first love is her home, and she knows how to manage money wisely. She invests in real estate and earns a profit from it. She takes that gain and reinvests it in agriculture. All of her business wisdom is used to profit the home. This is another reason the heart of the husband safely trusts in her.

"*She girdeth her loins with strength, and strengtheneth her arms*" (v. 17). This verse is not speaking of natural strength, but of spiritual strength. The virtuous woman is full of the Word of God. That's how she is able to accomplish all that she does—getting up early, going to get food, managing her business, planting a vineyard. The joy of the Lord is her strength.

"*She perceiveth that her merchandise is good: her candle goeth not out by night*" (v. 18). Do you recall what Solomon said about the "merchandise" of wisdom? He said it was better than that of silver. (Prov. 3:14.) The reference to her candle not going out refers to the times the virtuous woman stays awake far into the night tending to her business affairs and caring for the needs of her family. Solomon had this to say to us about Wisdom: "When thou liest down, thou shalt not be afraid: yea, thou shalt lie down, and thy sleep shall be sweet" (Prov. 3:24). Why? Because Wisdom is there to watch over us even as we take our rest.

Wisdom's Ministry—

"She layeth her hands to the spindle, and her hands hold the distaff. She stretcheth out her hand to the poor; yea, she reacheth forth her hands to the needy" (vv. 19,20). This woman ministers both to her family and to the downtrodden. She works in the home and outside the home. Even while she cares for her own loved ones, her hand is always open to uplift those in need.

Wisdom's Righteousness—

"She is not afraid of the snow for her household: for all her household are clothed with scarlet" (v. 21). Note this word "scarlet." It is an interesting word. Most of the time in the Old Testament, the Hebrew word translated "scarlet" is *towla* (or *tola*). *Towla* is actually the name of a worm, the crimson grub. What does a worm have to do with clothing or a covering or protection for the family?

The Tola was the rarest of all worms in the ancient world. It was under special protection of the Crown; only a few select persons were allowed to collect these creatures. Because the blood of the Tola was a unique shade of crimson. When the worm was crushed, the blood was extracted to make a special dye reserved exclusively for coloring the robes of the king and his family. Thus only royalty wore "scarlet."

In Psalm 22:6 David said prophetically of Jesus: "...I am a worm, and no man; a reproach of men, and despised of the people." The word "worm" in this verse is *towla*. This scripture is a reference to the crucifixion, when Jesus hung upon the cross and was held in contempt by the people.

So when Jesus (through David) said, "I am a 'Tola'," He meant that when He went to the cross, He would be crushed by the weight of our sins. But when His blood came out, then we could walk away free from all sin, clothed in "scarlet," in the garments of kings!

So verse 21 is saying that the household of the virtuous woman is clothed with the righteousness of God. That's why she doesn't fear the snow. She knows no plague can come near her dwelling. She has clothed her family in robes of righteousness.

Wisdom's Beauty—

"She maketh herself coverings of tapestry; her clothing is silk and purple" (v. 22). This verse makes it clear that it is all right for the woman of God to dress nicely, even expensively. The virtuous woman here wears silk and purple. Both of these are terms which denote richness of material and design. You will remember that purple was one of the special colors designated by God to be used by the children of Israel in the construction of the tabernacle in the wilderness. Judges 8:26 speaks of the "purple raiment that was on the *kings* of Midian." The story Jesus told about Lazarus and the rich man began with these words: "There was a certain *rich* man, which was clothed in *purple* and fine linen..." (Luke 16:19). In Acts 16:14 we met Lydia, a prosperous businesswoman who made her living as "a seller of purple." Silk was also a prized commodity. Besides its natural beauty, since it was spun by silkworms, it was made all the more valuable and desirable by its scarcity. It was so scarce, in fact, that this is one of only four references made to silk in the entire Bible. And it is the *virtuous* woman who is clothed in it, not the adulteress or the harlot!

Wisdom's Contribution—

"Her husband is known in the gates, when he sitteth among the elders of the land" (v. 23). Solomon says of Wisdom: "Exalt her, and she shall promote thee: she shall bring thee to honour..." (Prov. 4:8). Verse 23 illustrates the truth of that statement. The expression "in the gates" refers to the commercial, political and religious center of the city, the place where the "elders" or officials meet to carry on the affairs of state and society. Thus we see that the husband of the virtuous woman is a respected member of that select and honored group of men. One of the reasons he enjoys the esteem of his peers is because he has a wife of intelligence, charm and character, one known for her astute business sense as well as her regal beauty and social graces. Besides being a model wife and homemaker, this woman is a definite asset to her husband's career. When he brings business associates or clients home with him, he knows he can count on her to have the house immaculately clean and orderly, to have the table set with their finest dinnerware, to have prepared a delicious and eye-pleasing meal, to be dressed and groomed tastefully, and to entertain their guests with warmth, good humor and enthusiasm. What man would not be the envy of the whole city when blessed with such a life partner as that?

Wisdom's Vestments—

"She maketh fine linen.... Strength and honour are her clothing; and she shall rejoice in time to come" (vv. 24,25). Even if you are not able to outfit your wife in purple and silk right now, if you two will remain faithful to God and His Word, one day she will be dressed in the finest. Until that day, continue to emphasize the clothing of the "inward man." The virtuous woman will be found robed in righteousness and clothed with strength and honor. Her vestments will be those of a wise and learned counselor.

"She openeth her mouth with wisdom; and in her tongue is the law of kindness" (v. 26). Her testimony is:

"Counsel is mine, and sound wisdom: I am understanding; I have strength. By me kings reign, and princes decree justice. By me princes rule, and nobles, even all the judges of the earth" (Prov. 8:24).

Wisdom's Devotion—

"She looketh well to the ways of her household, and eateth not the bread of idleness" (v.27). Solomon says of this woman: "Wisdom hath builded her house.... She hath killed her beasts; she hath mingled her wine; she hath also furnished her table" (Prov. 9:1,2). The virtuous woman is a "home maker," not a "home breaker." She takes care of her own family, she doesn't waste her days meddling in other people's personal affairs. She is not idle but takes pleasure in seeing to the needs of her own household, the ones "nearest and dearest" to her. She puts her family first, knowing that her efforts are not in vain, but are investments in their future, seeds that will one day produce a harvest of joy.

Wisdom's Reward—

"Her children arise up, and call her blessed, her husband also, and he praiseth her: Many daughters have done virtuously, but thou excellest them all" (vv. 28,29). The *New International Version* makes this passage a little clearer: "Her children arise and call her blessed; her husband also, and he praises her: 'Many women do noble things, but you surpass them all.'" Have you ever heard a wife or mother express her frustration to her family in these words? "I work my fingers to the bone around here, and this is the reward I get!" This is not the testimony of Wisdom, the virtuous woman.

Wisdom tells us that she was created by God before anything else existed in the universe, that she was with Him at the time of creation, "when he appointed the foundations of the earth" (Prov. 8:29). Notice her next utterance: "Then I was by him, as one brought up with him: *and I was daily his delight, rejoicing always before him*" (v. 30). Wisdom has her reward. Wisdom delights God. Wisdom rejoices before Him—always!

"Favour is deceitful, and beauty is vain; but a woman that feareth the Lord, she shall be praised" (v. 30). The woman of wisdom, the righteous woman, will receive her due reward. Her children will arise and call her blessed, and her husband will praise her. But that's not all. Even the world will praise her.

"Give her of the fruit of her hands; and let her own works praise her in the gates" (v. 31). These "gates" are the same gates in which the husband found honor and esteem. There is coming a day when all of the sacrifices this virtuous woman has made on behalf of her family and her God will be repaid to her by the Lord. He will cause her to have favor with God and man. Peter speaks of husbands "giving honour unto the wife" (1 Pet. 3:7). And Solomon says in Proverbs 11:16 that "a gracious woman retaineth honour." God Himself will honor the virtuous woman. And when He does, it will not be a fleeting or transient honor. She will retain it. One day she will harvest the reward of what she has sown all through the years, the "fruit of her hands." Her own works will bring her praise and honor. God has promised it: "The wise shall inherit glory..." (Prov. 3:35). The wise woman will glory in her reward!

Who Can Find a Virtuous Woman?—

If you are a husband, you might be thinking: "How can I get my wife to be like that?" In Ephesians 5 the Apostle Paul tells us that the Church is the bride of Christ. Now when you and I became Christians, we became a part of that Church—a part of the bride. But right at that moment we did not look exactly like the a bride. Certainly not the Bride of the Lord Jesus Christ. We had weaknesses and faults and blemishes. We still do. Yet through the years we have come closer and closer to becoming what the Lord has in mind for us to be. How is that? What has caused this transformation we are undergoing? How does the Lord go about transforming His bride into the image He has of her in His mind and heart? The answer is found in Ephesians 5:25-28:

"Husbands, love your wives, even as Christ loved the church, and gave himself for it;

"That he might sanctify and cleanse it with the washing of water by the word,

"That he might present it to himself a glorious church, not having spot, or wrinkle, or any such thing; but that it should be holy and without blemish.

"So ought men to love their wives as their own bodies. He that loveth his wife loveth himself."

Jesus Christ transforms His Bride by cleansing us "with the washing of the water by the word" (v. 26). The Greek word translated "word" in this passage is *rhema*, which Strong defines as *"an utterance."* Jesus washes us with the SPOKEN Word. He never speaks what He SEES, but rather He speaks what He BELIEVES. That is the answer for us too.

Her Husband Praiseth Her—

So how do you get your wife to be that virtuous woman? Start praising her. Did you know that dirty water will not cleanse a person? Then neither does griping, yelling or complaining "cleanse" your wife. If she doesn't measure up to the standard set forth in Proverbs 31, don't criticize her for it, just love her. Love will change the wrong.

Exactly how do you go about loving your wife into the image of the virtuous woman? Jesus transforms His bride by continually washing us with good confessions. So in order to help you bring about the transformation you would like to see in your wife, I have paraphrased Proverbs 31:10-31 into a confession to be repeated out loud. Use this confession as a statement of faith. Speak it forth daily, believing that according to Mark 11:23,24 what you say will come to pass. As you speak, visualize in your mind the precise image you have for her. If you will be persistent—and patient!—sooner or later you will see your wife become exactly what you say.

(Husband, a word of caution: Be prepared. This confession goes to work on *your* attitude where many of her problems begin. Your duty is to love your wife as Christ loves the Church.)

Just Say the Word—

"I have found in my wife a virtuous woman. Her price is far above rubies.

"My heart safely trusts in her, and I lack nothing of value.

"She does me good and not evil, all the days of my life.

"She sees to it that our children are clothed in the finest, and she goes to the farthest limits to find the best food at the best prices.

"She is not lazy in preparing food for our family.

"Since the joy of the Lord is her strength, she is wise in business.

"The merchandise of her reward is good to her, and she does not become weary in well doing.

"Her love reaches also to the poor, expecting nothing of them in return.

"I fear no storm or adversity that might come against our family because she has seen that each one of us is covered with the robe of righteousness.

"She dresses herself in the finest. I am proud to be seen with her at all times.

"Because of her virtue and ability, I am more successful in my business. I have the respect of those in authority.

"She has clothed herself with strength and honor.

"I will rejoice with her for the rest of our lives. Her tongue speaks with wisdom and her mouth is filled with kindness.

"She looks after her household well. She is not idle.

"When the children rise up in the morning, they call her blessed. I praise her also.

"Outward beauty fades away, but she grows more beautiful every day because she fears the Lord.

"The rewards of her faithfulness will bring her the praise of those in the world. She will enjoy favor with God and man.

"There are many virtuous women, but my wife excels them all."

10

Friends

Proverbs 18:24; 27:6-19

In the preceding lessons we met and identified the woman known as Wisdom. We saw how the virtuous woman of Proverbs 31 is the sum total of all the wisdom of God wrapped up in one person. She is beautiful, intelligent, and personable. She is a good steward of God's blessings, capable in business and gifted in handling finances. She is an asset to her husband's career. She lends a helping hand to the poor and needy, and cares for her family with industry and thrift. She is a model homemaker, bringing her children up in the nurture and admonition of the Lord. In short, this woman called Wisdom combines everything needful for successful living.

In this lesson let's examine the book of Proverbs to discover what Wisdom has to say to us about how to cultivate successful friendships. As we do so, we will recall that the secret to success in any venture is to remember that success is a not an end in itself; rather it is a by-product of Godly living. As Christians, our primary purpose in life is not to achieve success, but to honor God and serve Him; if we will seek first His kingdom and His righteousness, success will follow as a matter of course. With that thought in mind, let's see what the Word of God would say to us about friendship.

Friendship Requires Discipline—

PROVERBS 18:24

A man that hath friends must show himself friendly: and there is a friend that sticketh closer than a brother.

Here is the formula for getting and keeping good friends. It is one thing to find a good wife, it is another thing to build a happy and harmonious marriage. It is one thing to find a friend, it is another thing to keep that friendship strong and healthy. In both cases, it takes *work*. That's why many friendships today are coming apart at the seams; for the same reason that so many modern marriages are ending in the divorce court. Simply because people have become lax and self-indulgent. They expect something for nothing. They expect the other person to do all the giving. For a marriage or a friendship to "work," each of the partners in that relationship must "work."

Christians today have become lazy. They have forgotten that the Christian lifestyle is one of discipline—*self*-discipline. It requires diligence and self-denial. In order to have friends, a person must learn to give as well as to take.

Cultivating a friendship is like cultivating any other crop. We reap what we sow. A good harvest depends on good seed sown in good ground. In order to get something out of the ground, we have to first put something into it. It takes time and effort to till the soil—this means taking the time to take an interest in someone other than our own self. We sow the seed of friendship by showing ourselves friendly. No farmer waits for the soil to come to him, he goes to it. He takes the initiative to see that that ground produces. Friendship must be as carefully cultivated as any other crop. Once the seed of friendship is sown, it must be constantly tended. It must be carefully watered, and the weeds must be removed. We water a friendship by intercessory prayer. We weed it by removing from our minds and hearts any thoughts of judgment—hurt feelings, jealousy, envy, mistrust or animosity—we might have toward our friend. If we will do that, we will reap a bountiful harvest from our friendship.

The world is starving for friendship today because people are waiting for the other person to do the tilling, sowing, watering and weeding. Wisdom would say to such people, "In order to have friends, you must pay the price of friendship; you must make *yourself* a friend!"

Types of Friends—

When Wisdom speaks to us about friends, she is not talking just about mere acquaintances or neighbors. She is not referring just to someone we live next door to or someone we occasionally chat with on the street. Her remarks also have to do with true friendship, that close bond that exists between two people whose hearts and minds are blended together as were those of David and Jonathan in the Old Testament: "And it came to pass, when he (David) had made an end of speaking unto Saul, that the soul of Jonathan was knit with the soul of David, and Jonathan loved him as his own soul" (1 Sam. 18:1).

There are several words in the Old Testament Hebrew that have been translated into the *King James Version* as "friend." Two of these are of special interest to us because they differ significantly. In Proverbs 18:24, the word "friends" is the Hebrew word *rea'*, which means "an *associate*:....neighbour..." (*Strong*). Likewise the adjective "friendly" in that verse is derived from a word meaning (among other things) "to *associate* with (as friend)." But the final word translated "friend" in Proverbs 18:24 (the "friend that sticketh closer than a brother") is the Hebrew word *'ahab*, which is from a primitive root word meaning "to *have affection for.*" So there is a pronounced difference between the two types of "friends" mentioned in the Old Testament: between a **rea'** (a neighbor, someone with whom we *associate*) and a **'ahab** (a friend, someone with whom we share real *affection*), as did David and Jonathan ("...and Jonathan *loved him* as his own soul").

So this verse is telling us that if we want to have a "friend" (*rea'*, a neighbor), then we must show ourselves "friendly" (neighborly). But then it goes on to say that there is a FRIEND (*'ahab*), a true friend, one who loves us as his own soul) who will stick to us closer than a brother.

The point being made here is that friendship is based upon *mutual* relationship. If we expect others to be friendly to us, we must be friendly to them. This is an Old Testament equivalent to the New Testament admonition: "Therefore all things whatsoever ye would that men should do to you, do ye even so to them: for this is the law and the prophets" (Matt. 7:12). The "law" to which our Lord referred here includes the spiritual law of sowing and reaping. He was thus telling us just what Wisdom has been declaring for ages: "If you want to HAVE friends, you must BE a friend. You will REAP what you SOW."

Value of Friendship—

"Two are better than one; because they have a good reward for their labour.

"For if they fall, the one will lift up his fellow: but woe to him that is alone when he falleth; for he hath not another to help him up.

"Again, if two lie together, then they have heat: but how can one be warm alone?

"And if one prevail against him, two shall withstand him; and a threefold cord is not quickly broken" (Eccl. 4:9-12).

At one certain time in his life, wise Solomon made a mistake. He got out of fellowship with God. He turned from the spiritual to the natural. He tried the things of the world to see if they would fill the hunger and quench the dryness he felt in his soul. He attempted to fill a spiritual void with natural material. Of course, his efforts were not successful.

In the book of Ecclesiastes we have a record, a sort of diary or journal, of Solomon's experiment. We need to read and understand this book in that context. That way we will gain knowledge and wisdom even from what has been described as "a morbid piece of literature." Despite its pessimistic conclusions, Ecclesiastes does not have to be depressing. Through Solomon's worldly experiences we can gain new insight into the world in general and into our own selves in particular. Let's examine what Solomon had to say here in this passage about friendship. It represents one of the few positive truths he shares with us in this book.

"Two are better than one:..." (v. 9a). We often say that two heads are better than one; and that's usually true. It is a spiritual principle like sowing and reaping. Jesus said that if any two shall agree on earth as touching anything they shall ask, it shall be done for them of the Father. (Matt. 18:19.) Perhaps that is the reason Jesus sent out His disciples in pairs. (Luke 10:1.) If the scriptural principle of Deuteronomy 32:20 holds true, one could put a thousand demons to flight, but two could chase away ten thousand! In any case, two is a good number to be:

"...because they have a good reward for their labour" (v. 9b). Of course, this has reference to the fact that one person can help the other if he falls. Two together can give warmth one to the other. But it can also be taken in this sense, that friendship takes joint effort. It takes labor to build a friendship. Why? Because friends don't always get along. Yet many times the very thing that seems to drive them apart is the very thing that brought them together in the first place: They are *alike*. That's why brothers often fight worse than any other two people on earth. Because, like Adam and Eve, they are flesh of the same flesh, and bone of the same bone. As in the case of David and Jonathan, really close friends are of one soul. And there is usually no one with whom we are more often at odds than our own self. But there is also no other human who knows us better.

Other than the Lord Jesus Christ, our best friend on earth should be our spouse. Because when two people are joined together in holy matrimony, in the eyes of the Lord the two become one. (Matt. 19:5,6.) If you aren't friends with your "other self," then you're in trouble. If you can't confide in your "better half," then who can you trust?

That's why I don't believe in love at first sight. True and lasting love doesn't just suddenly "happen"; it develops over a period of time. Marriage is not really built on love; at least, not the kind of sentimental or sensual love portrayed so often on the screen or in cheap romance novels. The foundation for truly successful marriage is friendship. True love grows out of true friendship: "Greater love hath no man that this, that a man lay down his life for his friends. Ye are my friends..." (John 15:14). If two people are not friends when they get married, or if they stop being friends after they are married, their marriage is destined for trouble.

"*And if one prevail against him, two shall withstand him;...*" (v. 12a). This is an important truth. It emphasizes the fact that any enemy who comes against me must also come against my friend, my wife, my "other self." Because we are one.

"*...and a threefold cord is not quickly broken*" (v. 12b). Notice that this friendship is actually a *three*fold cord. Something has been added to it to give it additional strength to withstand the pressures of life. That third strand is Jesus Christ. If the two friends are Christians, then He can become one with them. With His divine presence and help, that friendship, that marriage, will stand. The very gates of hell shall not be able to prevail against it!

A Friend Corrects—

PROVERBS 27:6

Faithful are the wounds of a friend; but the guises
of an enemy are deceitful.

Watch out for those people who always praise you. They may be your enemy in disguise. In Luke 6:26 Jesus told His disciples, "Woe unto you, when all men shall speak well of you! for so did their fathers to the false prophets." In other words, our Lord warns us to beware of people who tell us that we can do no wrong.

No matter who we are, we all make mistakes. We miss the mark from time to time. No one is infallible or immune to error. Spiritually, in our inner man, we Christians are the righteousness of God in Christ; that is true. But at the same time it must be noted that our outward man is still catching up, still learning to *become* what we have been declared by God to *be*. Like a young man who is crowned king by proclamation yet who must then learn to fulfill the duties and responsibilities of a ruling monarch, so we the children of God must learn to conduct ourselves in a manner worthy of the title we bear.

In learning to be perfect even as our Father in heaven is perfect, we need people to be honest with us. To counsel and advise us. To inform us when we begin to get out of line. If everyone always tells us that everything we do is wonderful, we will never improve. That's why we need a true friend who will "level" with us about ourselves.

Notice that this verse says that the wounds a friend may inflict upon us are *faithful*. Why would a friend "wound" us? Precisely because he IS our friend. A friend wounds us because he loves us. Love is kind, but it is also honest. It doesn't gloss over the truth or excuse wrong doing just to keep someone happy. God is love, but God is also just. So is a true friend. And, like it or not, sometimes the truth does hurt. But then, growth is always painful. Putting away childish things is not always easy or pleasant. Becoming a man, developing maturity, requires discipline and correction. So when a friend wounds us, it is for our own good. His purpose is not to harm us but to guide us back to the straight and narrow way that leads to life. And that itself is not easy; one of the hardest things in life is to have to tell someone you love that he is wrong. But a true friend will do that; he will speak up when the one he loves is about to get into trouble or is heading in the wrong direction.

Solomon tells us in Proverbs 28:23: "He that rebuketh a man afterwards shall find more favour than he that flattereth with the tongue." At the time, the hardest thing in the world to do is to rebuke a friend. But notice that this verse says that afterwards the one who does that will have more favor than the one who flatters. If we are sensitive and caring at all, we are hesitant to correct our friends. We don't want to offend them or to jeopardize our friendship. That's why we must carefully examine our motives. If we avoid correcting a friend we know to be in the wrong simply because we are too timid or afraid, we are not being a true friend. On the other hand, we should not be too hasty or brash about setting other people straight. There is a balance that must be maintained here. But if our motives are honest and we act out of sincere love, then we will not cause harm either to the friend or the friendship. In the end, both will be strengthened. And we will enjoy more favor with our friend than if we had kept silent or resorted to flattery.

A Friend Counsels—

VERSE 9

Ointment and perfume rejoice the heart: so doth
the sweetness of a man's friend by hearty counsel.

When a friend counsels us, it may not be pleasant at the moment. But if that counsel motivates us to move in the right direction, if it proves to be well founded and results in success, then we're glad we followed their advice. What may have been repulsive, now has become a "sweet smelling savour" to us.

A Friend Supports—

VERSE 10

Thine own friend, and thy father's friend, forsake
not; neither go into thy brother's house in the day

of calamity: for better is a neighbour that is near than a brother far off.

Have you ever forsaken an old friend when a new one came along? Did you feel guilty for doing so? When you make new friends, don't slight your old ones. Wisdom also counsels not to forsake the friends of your father. That means the previous generation. Some of the wisest counsel you can receive is from the older generation. Because the old folks have lived though hard times and can tell you how to survive.

Why is it so important to have friends? The second part of this verse answers that question. Blood relatives may live far off and not be able to help in time of need. But a friend who lives nearby will always be close enough to lend a helping hand. He is there to stand with you in times of crisis and to lend daily support rather than long-distance well-wishing.

A Friend Sharpens—

VERSE 17

Iron sharpeneth iron; so a man sharpeneth the countenance of his friend.

When you and your best friend get together, do you sometimes "rub each other the wrong way"? If so, you are helping him and he's helping you. There are times when we need to be "rubbed the wrong way." Without it, we get dull...like an axe that has been used too long. An axe isn't sharpened with softsoap; it takes a whetstone. So when you get with your friend and "sparks start to fly," don't worry about it. You can't grind an axe without giving off sparks. That's what God gave us good friends for—to keep us sharp.

Think about this for a moment: Do you think it is wise to have lots of close friends? No, it's not. Friends are like salt, a little goes a long way; just the right amount adds zest and brings out the flavor, too much spoils the stew. If you will stop and reflect on it, you probably have one or maybe two truly close friends, people you can really confide in. That's enough.

Even Jesus in His natural life didn't have a large number of close friends. Out of the twelve disciples, only three were really close to Him—Peter, James and John. Of these, John seems to have been the closest to the Lord. So in reality, Jesus probably had one really intimate friend in this world. Which may explain why some of the others were sometimes jealous.

It is a sign of insecurity to have a lot of friends. Often it indicates that the person has no confidence in himself, that he has to depend on the support and approval of others.

Thank God for one or two close friends. In the long run, that's all a man really needs. They will be there, rain or shine, good times or bad, when he's up or when he's down. That means a lot.

A Friend Reflects—

VERSE 19

As in water face answereth to face, so the heart of man to man.

In the days of the ancient world, water was recognized as a reflector of reality. Today we rely on mirrors. One thing about a mirror is its integrity. Like a camera, it doesn't lie. A mirror will not flatter you at all. It shows you exactly as you are. If your hair is standing on end, the mirror won't spare your feelings by picturing you with every hair in place. It does not create an image, it just reflects the image of whatever is placed in front of it.

That's what a good friend does. He reveals to us our flaws and faults so we can correct them, just as we comb our hair because we see in a mirror that it needs it. If we are to correct our faults, we must first know that we have faults and what they are. So a good friend, like a good mirror, actually does us a service by helping us to see ourselves as we really are, rather than allowing us a distorted image of what we would like to think we are. A true friend is truthful. And truth is one of our best friends, because it is the truth that sets us free! (John 8:32.)

The True Friend—

You may be thinking that you don't have a good, close friend. Maybe you haven't taken the time to build a close friendship with anyone. In fact, you may not have any friends at all that you can think of. Your life may be lonely and miserable. If so, what can you do about it? Where do you begin?

We began our study of friends by examining Proverbs 18:24: "A man that hath friends must show himself friendly: and there is a friend that sticketh closer than a brother." The first half of that scripture tells you where to begin, what to do to develop true human friendships. Put it into practice and you will have friends.

But it is the second half of that scripture that actually holds the most promise of lasting friendship on this earth: "*...there is a friend that sticketh closer than a brother.*" Despite what you may think, you do have a Friend. Someone went to a great deal of effort and expense to make you His friend. In fact, before the foundation of the earth was laid, this Person purposely devised a plan for you to become His friend. He prized your friendship so much, He spared no expense, He went to the limit. He sent His own Son to die on the cross of Calvary to remove the barrier which separated you from Him. That barrier was sin. Now that that barrier has been removed by the blood of Christ, that Person invites you to become His friend.

If calamity and trouble have been so much a part of your life that it seems that everywhere you turn you are on the verge of falling, be strengthened in knowing that you have a Friend who stands by your side. When the enemy comes against you to destroy you, be assured that you have a Friend to protect and preserve you. When sickness and disease threaten, be comforted in the fact that your Friend has taken upon Himself all your pains and sorrows so that you can live in fullness of life. Whenever trials and tribulations come to cause you anxiety or distress, be still and know that your Friend is there to watch over you and that nothing shall by any means harm you.

Jesus, our best Friend, withstood our greatest enemy and defeated him. There is no calamity that can befall us that we and Jesus together cannot handle. If you have never met this Friend, do so right now. You'll never regret it. Because He is the Friend who sticks closer than a brother.

11
Neighbors
Proverbs 3:3,4; 17:17; 22:11-25;
25:8-20; 27:14; 26:18,19

When the book of Proverbs talks about "neighbours," it does not refer to those people who live on either side of you, or down the street. These neighbors are those whom you have a like fellowship with. And it is good to have plenty of fellowships like that. Generally the more good neighbors you have, the better. Because you can help each other out individually and, as a group you can band together to get more accomplished than any one of you could alone. But these are not the intimate, close friends we spoke of in our last lesson. Let's see then what Wisdom would say to us about neighbors.

Love Thy Neighbour—

"Then one of them, which was a lawyer, asked him a question, tempting him, and saying,

"Master, which is the great commandment in the law?

"Jesus said unto him, Thou shalt love the Lord thy God with all thy heart, and with all thy soul, and with all thy mind.

"This is the first and great commandment.

"And the second is like unto it, Thou shalt love thy neighbour as thyself.

"On these two commandments hang all the law and the prophets" (Matt. 22:35-40).

In Romans 13:9 the Apostle Paul tells us that all the commandments can be summed up in the words, "...Thou shalt love thy neighbour as thyself." Then in the next verse he goes on to tell us why: "Love worketh no ill to his neighbour: therefore love is the fulfilling of the law."

Then in Galatians, Paul states: "For all the law is fulfilled in one word, even in this; Thou shalt love thy neighbour as thyself."

According to the scriptures, if we keep that one commandment, we won't break any of the rest of them. Which seems reasonable. If we love our neighbor, we won't steal from him, or defile his marriage by committing adultery with his wife, or bear false witness against him, or kill him, or do any other of those things against him which are expressly forbidden in the law. So if we love our neighbor, we will fulfill the law.

Under the New Covenant we are no longer subject to the law because the Holy Spirit now lives in us. He sheds abroad in our heart the love of God. (Rom. 5:5.) To "shed abroad" means to pour forth or to spill. So the love of God now pours forth or spills out of us upon ALL those around us.

It is significant that our Lord didn't command us to love our *friend* or our *brother*, but rather to love our *neighbor*— including our enemies: "For if ye love them which love you, what reward have ye? do not even the publicans the same? And if ye salute your brethren only, what more do ye than others? do not even the publicans so?" (Matt. 7:46,47). The New Testament Greek word translated "neighbour" in the *King James Version* has the connotation of "fellow." So in actuality Jesus was not saying, "Love the person who lives close to you," but rather, "Love your fellowman." And our fellowman includes everyone—neighbor, relative, friend, acquaintance, stranger, AND enemy.

How to Win Friends and Influence People—

In 2 Corinthians 5:18 Paul tells us that "God hath given to us the ministry of reconciliation." To "reconcile" means to bring into harmony with or to make friends with. As Christians, we are sent into all the world to preach "the word of reconciliation" (v. 19). Like Paul, "We are ambassadors for Christ" (v. 20). That is, our job is to go into all the world and preach reconciliation between man and God, to make friends between man and His Maker. We are to say to the world, *by our actions as much as by our words*, "We pray you in Christ's stead, be ye reconciled to God" (v. 20). One way we do that is by first bringing about reconciliation, making friends, between our fellowman and ourselves. There are several ways to make friends. Let's look at some of them.

Show Mercy—

PROVERBS 3:3,4

Let not mercy and truth forsake thee: bind them about thy neck; write them upon the table of thine heart:

So shalt thou find favour and good understanding in the sight of God and man.

Did you notice the title of our last section? "How to Win Friends and Influence People." We said that was what we were sent into the world to do, to win friends for God. One way we do that is by showing people the mercy and truth of the Lord. That gives us favor with them and with our Father. Then we can bring them into favor with Him. We can act as liaison, or ambassador, for Christ.

The Hebrew word translated "favour" in the *King James Version* of Proverbs 3:4 is the same Hebrew word translated "grace" throughout the Old Testament. A related word is translated "mercy" in verse 3. So this passage is telling us that if we show mercy (grace, favor), we will find favor (mercy, grace) with God and our fellowman. Again, the spiritual law of sowing and reaping in operation.

We know that we have favor with God. It was by His favor (grace) that we were born again. That same favor is upon all men; most of them just haven't yet availed themselves of it as we did. And the reason many of them haven't availed themselves of it is because they don't know about it. That's why they need to hear the "word of reconciliation." So they can benefit from it. That's the Good News we are sent out to share with them.

There is nothing better in all the world than to have favor with God through His Son, Jesus Christ. Nothing on earth can compare with having Jesus as your Friend, to walk daily in His grace and favor.

But we don't live just in a spirit world. We also live in a natural world. We also need favor with men. That too is a gift (grace, favor) from God, given to those who love and serve Him. As we are obedient to Him, as we become like Him, as we show mercy to others, we ourselves obtain mercy. We receive favor with men. So then the best way to make friends in this world is to show them the mercy, grace and favor of the Lord, to win them to Christ. As we make friends for Christ, we make friends for life.

Follow the Word, meditate in it, tie it about your neck. Share the Word (of reconciliation) with your neighbor, your fellowman. If you will do that, you will have favor with God, and favor with man. You will have more friends than you'll know what to do with.

Show Love—

PROVERBS 17:17

A friend loveth at all times, and a brother is born for adversity.

When you have a friend, he is true to you at *all* times, day or night. He may be closer to you than a relative. A brother or sister may be someone you call on only during a crisis. Rarely do brothers and sisters remain close after both are married. But "a friend loveth at *all* times."

Show Wisdom—

PROVERBS 22:11

He that loveth pureness of heart, for the grace of his lips the king shall be his friend.

This verse says that if we will walk in wisdom and holiness, speaking forth the grace of God, then we will have friends in high places. God rewards the faithful by granting them favor with those in positions of authority.

The negative side of this truth is illustrated by Proverbs 19:4: "Wealth maketh many friends; but the poor is separated from his neighbour." Meaning that many people depend upon their riches to buy friends for themselves, but such "friends" are unstable; they will disappear as soon as the money is gone. Proverbs 19:6 echoes the same idea: "Many will intreat the favour of the prince: and every man is a friend to him that giveth gifts." Everyone wants to be friends of the "high and mighty"; rich gifts always attract a crowd of admiring "friends." But they are not to be counted on, because their only interest is in advancing themselves. A true friend is interested in you, not your power or wealth.

As Christians we need to show wisdom in our dealings with people. The Word of God is the source of our friends, not our material wealth or high office. As we hold forth the Word of God, it will lead us to true friends who love us for ourselves and not for our possessions or position.

In making friends for the Lord and for ourselves, Wisdom tells us that there are some people we would do well to avoid. Let's see who some of these people are.

Avoid the Angry Man—

VERSES 24,25

Make no friendship with an angry man; and with a furious man thou shalt not go.

Lest thou learn his ways, and get a snare to thy soul.

Sometimes a person, even though Christian, can be full of bitterness. The love of God may seem to draw you to him in an attempt to help. But here the Bible warns to keep your defenses up. Make sure you don't become too involved with an angry, bitter man.

People who are bitter have a tendency to pour out the bitterness of their heart upon whoever will listen. They will tell you how they are being mistreated, how the church staff or other church members are using or abusing them. If you listen too long to such talk, sooner or later you will begin to believe all or part of it. You will unconsciously begin to pick up their negative attitude and outlook. If you sense that danger, break off the association. You can remain friends with that person from a distance, you can continue to pray for and with him. But don't allow yourself to be drawn into his despondency and pessimism. You will end up as bad as he is, or else he will end up hating you because you won't join him in his bitterness and animosity. Either way you will have lost your ability to minister to him.

Avoid the Impatient Man—

PROVERBS 25:8

Go not forth hastily to strive, lest thou know not what to do in the end thereof, when thy neighbour hath put thee to shame.

One of the greatest virtues among friends is patience. I have learned as a pastor that not everything is as it appears. Many times in counseling a couple, I will hear only one side of the story. The wife may give her viewpoint and it may seem that her husband is totally to blame for the sorry state of their marriage. But then when I hear her husband's testimony, the very opposite may seem to be the case; it may look like the wife is the guilty party. I have learned to reserve judgment until I have heard both sides of any situation. If I react too quickly after hearing only one side, I end up looking foolish and being put to shame when the whole story comes out. I can attest from experience that it is never wise to run off "half cocked."

In such cases, I have found that patience is the key. If I will hear both sides of the matter without allowing myself to become involved in the bitterness or strife of either, in time the truth will begin to manifest itself, either through the actions of the parties involved or by direct revelation from the Lord. That's why we are admonished by James to "let patience have her perfect work, that ye may be perfect and entire, wanting nothing" (James 1:4). Faith and patience always inherit the promises. (Heb. 6:12.)

Wisdom would tell us to avoid the impatient man as we avoid the angry man—and for the same reason. So we will not be influenced by his negative traits. Instead, if we will display faith and patience, we will find and win more friends for God and for ourselves.

Be Honest—

VERSE 9

Debate thy cause with thy neighbour himself; and discover not a secret to another.

If you are having trouble with one of your friends, you should be honest with him about it. Don't go around talking *about* him; go and talk directly *to* him. People might have something against me, but unless they come and tell me so, the only way I will know about it is through gossip. And that is not the best source of information for a Christian.

This verse tells us not only to go directly to our friend with our grievances, but also not to spread those grievances around to other people. If there are problems between us and our neighbor, we need to keep those problems between the parties involved. Peter tells us that love covers a multitude of sins. (1 Pet. 4:8.) If we are to win friends and keep their friendship, we must learn to overlook certain faults in them and concentrate our attention on their positive qualities.

Be Dependable—

VERSES 13,14,19

As the cold of snow in the time of harvest, so is a faithful messenger to them that send him: for he refresheth the soul of his masters.

Whoso boasteth himself of a false gift is like clouds and wind without rain....

Confidence in an unfaithful man in time of trouble is like a broken tooth, and a foot out of joint.

"As the cold of snow in the time of harvest, so is a faithful messenger to them that send him: for he refresheth the soul of his masters" (v. 13). A friend who is faithful, one who can always be counted on, is as refreshing as the first snow of winter. That's what we must be if we are to win friends for ourselves and our God. We must remember that the way to win friends is to be a friend. And a true friend is dependable.

"Confidence in an unfaithful man in time of trouble is like a broken tooth, and a foot out of joint" (v. 19). Unfaithfulness causes a friendship to be torn down. Can you think of anything more useless than a broken tooth when you are trying to eat? Can you think of anything more painful than a foot out of joint when you are trying to walk? That's how painful and aggravating an undependable person is to someone who has to rely on him.

"Whoso boasteth himself of a false gift is like clouds and wind without rain" (v. 19). As Christians, we dare not boast of a false gift. When we tell someone that we have the gift (the ability) to do something, that had better be the truth. But

not only must we be able to do what we have promised, we must then be certain we fulfill that promise. No one will win very many friends if he does not keep his word.

Be Considerate—

VERSES 17,20

Withdraw thy foot from thy neighbour's house; lest he be weary of thee, and so hate thee....

As he that taketh away a garment in cold weather, and as vinegar upon nitre, so is he that singeth songs to an heavy heart.

"Withdraw thy foot from thy neighbour's house; lest he be weary of thee, and so hate thee" (v. 17). There is no faster way to lose a friend than to wear out your welcome. Don't visit your friend's house too often or stay too long. Always leave your friends wanting more. That way they will truly be glad to see you next time. Make sure they never see enough of you by making sure they never see too much of you!

"As he that taketh away a garment in cold weather, and as vinegar upon nitre, so is he that singeth songs to a heavy heart" (v. 20). There are those who would tell us that as Christians we are to go around with a cheery smile on our face all the time, singing and shouting glory at the top of our lungs, slapping everyone on the back and telling them to cheer up and praise the Lord! And in Romans 12:15 Paul does counsel us to "rejoice with them that do rejoice..." But then in the second part of that verse he adds, "...and weep with them that weep." That doesn't mean that we are to take on their problems and become depressed with them. It just means that we are to be sensitive to the feelings and needs of others. While we are to lift people's spirits and encourage them, we are not to go around with a pat answer telling everyone we meet to put on a happy face. Beauty may be just skin deep, but most people's problems and hurts go much deeper than that.

What happens when you take off your jacket in cold weather? Your body reacts the moment it feels that numbing cold. And do you know what happens when vinegar hits "nitre" (soda)? It sets off a reaction. So does slapping someone on the back who is badly sunburned! So does singing "hallelujah choruses" to a neighbor who has just lost his wife or business. If we are foolish enough to do that, we will be the ones to lose. We will lose a friend.

Proverbs 27:14 says: "He that blesseth his friend with a loud voice, rising early in the morning, it shall be counted a curse to him." As Christians, we need to set a good example by being considerate of others.

In an earlier lesson we read this passage from Proverbs 26:18,19:

"As a mad man who casteth firebrands, arrows, and death,

"So is the man that deceiveth his neighbour, and saith, Am I not in sport?"

One of the quickest ways to lose friends is to be a practical joker. If you are a practical joker, it is a good sign you are insecure. Practical jokers don't have many real friends, only people who endure them. People just don't like to be the butt of a practical joke. They don't appreciate someone else making a spectacle of them. To the victim, no practical joke is much "sport." In the Old Testament, Samson was a practical joker. How many friends did Samson have? None. That ought to be a lesson to us. We can't expect to win friends for the kingdom by being inconsiderate of other people.

Who Is My Neighbour?—

"And, behold, a certain lawyer stood up, and tempted him saying, Master, what shall I do to inherit eternal life?

"He said unto him, What is written in the law? how readest thou?

"And he answering said, Thou shalt love the Lord thy God with all thy heart, and with all thy soul, and with all thy strength, and with all thy mind; and thy neighbour as thyself.

"And he said unto him, Thou hast answered right: this do, and thou shalt live.

"But he, willing to justify himself, said unto Jesus, And who is my neighbour?" (Luke 10:25-29).

At the beginning of this lesson, we read a passage from the Gospel of Matthew in which a lawyer asked the Lord Jesus a question, trying to "tempt" Him: "Master, what is the great commandment in the law?" (Matt. 22:35). Now in this familiar passage we see that Jesus is questioned by "a certain lawyer" who wanted to "tempt" Him into saying something he could take issue with. There is some evidence that this is the same incident, just related a little differently by Luke. In Matthew's version the lawyer asks which is the "great commandment." Luke has Jesus asking the lawyer a question. In any case, it's the answer which interests us most in our study. Here the lawyer indicated that the law requires a man to love God totally—and his neighbor as himself. When Jesus agreed with him, the lawyer was not satisfied. Still trying to justify his own lack of love, the nimble-minded lawyer came up with another question: "And who is my neighbour?" (v. 29).

Now Jesus could have given the response we gave earlier in this lesson, "Neighbor means fellowman; you are to love everybody." But if He had said that, the lawyer would likely have replied, "But how can I love everybody? I don't know everybody." So rather than answering directly, Jesus told a parable to illustrate His meaning. Let's look at it.

Which of These Was Neighbour?—

"And Jesus answering said, A certain man went down from Jerusalem to Jericho, and fell among thieves, which stripped him of his raiment, and wounded him, and departed, leaving him half dead.

"And by chance there came down a certain priest that way: and when he saw him, he passed by on the other side.

"And likewise a Levite, when he was at the place, came and looked on him, and passed by on the other side.

"But a certain Samaritan, as he journeyed, came where he was: and when he saw him, he had compassion on him,

"And went to him, and bound up his wounds, pouring in oil and wine, and set him on his own beast, and brought him to an inn, and took care of him.

"And on the morrow when he departed, he took out two pence, and gave them to the host, and said unto him, Take care of him; and whatsoever thou spendest more, when I come again, I will repay thee.

"Which now of these three, thinkest thou, was neighbour unto him that fell among the thieves?

"And he said, He that shewed mercy on him. Then said Jesus unto him, Go, and do thou likewise" (vv. 30-37).

Now this story is very significant. It is an allegory, each of the people and events portrayed in it are symbolic. The man lying in the road represents Adam, or man. As Adam was traveling on his way, he fell among thieves. Who is the thief in John 10:10 who comes to steal, kill and destroy? Satan. In verse 30 we see that the enemy did three things to this man (representing the three curses of the law): 1) "Stripped him of his raiment" (representing poverty); 2) "Wounded him" (representing physical sickness); and, 3) "Departed, leaving him half dead" (representing spiritual death). "Half dead" means that he was dead spiritually, but still alive physically.

The first two people who came by but who were of no help to the man are also symbolic. The priest of verse 31 is a type of the law. The Levite in verse 32 is a type of the ritual of the law. This signifies that neither the law nor rituals can save a person.

Next came the person known to us today as the Good Samaritan. Can you guess what he symbolizes? He is the Savior.

Now let me ask you something. When the lawyer asked the Lord what he should do to inherit eternal life, Jesus agreed with him that if he would love God with all his being and love his neighbor as himself, he would live. Is that so? Jesus told a parable which *seemed* to illustrate the point that loving one's neighbor was enough to qualify a person for heaven. Can a person really inherit eternal life by loving his neighbor? Do you think that if you just love your next door neighbor that is enough to save you? Is loving the man who works next to you on the job all it takes for you to enter the kingdom of God? No, I don't think you believe that. Neither do I. We both know that loving our neighbor will not get us into heaven. Religious people have tried that for years; it just doesn't work.

As a boy, when I used to hear that parable taught in Sunday School, I thought the message was to go out and help people. Find someone in need and show them love. Now that is good, but it is not the principle of this parable. The question the lawyer asked originally was, "And who is my neighbour?" (v. 29). But the question Jesus asked at the end of His parable was, "Which of these, thinkest thou, was neighbour unto him that fell among the thieves?" (v. 37.) Do you see the difference? The neighbor was not the man on the road who *needed* help; the neighbor was the man who *provided* the help! And who was he? Who was neighbor to the man in need?

What did we say earlier in this lesson? We are to do unto others as we would have them do unto us. Why? Let's put it another way. Why are we to love our neighbor—our fellowman—as ourselves? Because in a very real sense he IS us! And we are him!

But there is more to it than that. We also said that even though we are to love others as ourselves, no one can be saved by loving others. How then are we saved? "Thou shalt love *the Lord thy God* with all thy heart, and with all thy strength, and with all thy mind..." (v. 27). There is only one Person we can love that will get us into heaven.

Who was neighbor to the man who fell among thieves? "He that shewed mercy on him" (v. 37). The Good Samaritan. So then the Good Samaritan might better be called the Good Neighbor! Who did we say the Good Samaritan represented? The Savior. So then when we love our NEIGHBOR as ourself, who do we love? We love the Lord JESUS! "Inasmuch as ye have done it unto the least of these my brethren, ye have done it unto me" (Matt. 25:31). It is by loving, serving, believing in Him that we are saved: "Believe on the Lord Jesus Christ, and thou shalt be saved..." (Acts 16:31). It was this same Jesus, this same Good Neighbor, who showed mercy on us when we had fallen among thieves. "Beloved, if God so loved us, we ought also to love one another" (1 John 4:11). So that's why we should love our neighbor as ourself. Not just because he IS us. But because God first loved us and gave Himself for us, and because He tells us, "Go, and do thou likewise." Now we are to be the GOOD NEIGHBOR.

Bob Yandian, Pastor of Grace Fellowship in Tulsa, Oklahoma, has an anointing and extensive teaching background that enables him to convey the uncompromised Word of God with an everyday practical clarity. Primarily, Bob ministers to students of the Word — fellow full-time ministers, congregational members, and Bible school students.

A graduate of Trinity Bible College, Bob studied under its director and founder, Charles Duncombe, a contemporary and companion of Smith Wigglesworth. Bob also studied Greek at Southwestern College in Oklahoma City.

In 1972 Bob began teaching regularly at Grace Fellowship where he was a founding member. In 1973 he began working for Kenneth Hagin Ministries as Tape Production Manager then, in 1977, for Rhema Bible Training Center as a teacher. Later he became Dean of Instructors. In 1980 he began pastoring Grace Fellowship.

Bob has taught and ministered throughout the United States and Canada, in South Africa, Guatemala, and the Philippines. He has spoken at numerous Full Gospel Businessmen's Fellowship International meetings; the Greater Pittsburgh Charismatic Conference; Bill Basansky's 1981, 1982, and 1983 jubilees; Salt Lake Institute of Religion (Mormon); and hosted the Local Church Seminar at Grace Fellowship.

To receive Bob Yandian's newsletter,
write:

Bob Yandian
P. O. Box 35842
Tulsa, OK 74153

*Feel free to include your prayer requests
and comments when you write.*

BOOKS AND CASSETTE TAPES
by Bob Yandian

Cassette Tapes

The Psalms of Moses
One Flesh
The Life of Moses
The Rapture Question
Galatians
Ephesians
Life of Christ
A Better Covenant
Sermon on the Mount
Joshua

The Chastening of the Lord
Proverbs
Prosperity
Psalms of Deliverance
Church Government
Romans
The Fruit of Love
The Kingdom Parables
The Local Church

God's Word to Pastors: Acts 20
Hebrews 11: God's Hall of Fame

Books

Joel: The Outpouring of God's Glory

Galatians: The Spirit Controlled Life

Ephesians: The Maturing of the Saints

Resurrection: Our Victory Over Death

The Holy Spirit: Oil & Wine

How to Become Great in the Kingdom of God

The Local Church

Available from your local bookstore.

HARRISON HOUSE
P. O. Box 35035
Tulsa, OK 74153